Unloved

Also by Toni Maguire

Don't Tell Mummy
When Daddy Comes Home
Helpless
Nobody Came
Don't You Love Your Daddy?
Can't Anyone Help Me?
Pretty Maids All In A Row
They Stole My Innocence
Did You Ever Love Me?
Daddy's Little Girl
Silent Child
Please Protect Us
No Going Home
Won't You Love Me?
Why Father?
An Innocent Child

Unloved

Can Marc ever escape his childhood?

TONI MAGUIRE

with Marc Clegg

First published in the UK by John Blake Publishing
An imprint of Bonnier Books UK
5th Floor, HYLO, 103–105 Bunhill Row,
London, EC1Y 8LZ

Owned by Bonnier Books
Sveavägen 56, Stockholm, Sweden

Paperback – 978-1-789-467-63-5
eBook – 978-1-789-467-64-2

All rights reserved. No part of the publication may be reproduced, stored in a retrieval system, transmitted or circulated in any form or by any means, electronic, mechanical, photocopying, recording or otherwise, without prior permission in writing from the publisher.

A CIP catalogue of this book is available from the British Library.

Design by www.envydesign.co.uk
Printed and bound in Great Britain by Clays Ltd, Elcograf S.p.A.

1 3 5 7 9 10 8 6 4 2

Copyright © Toni Maguire and Marc Clegg, 2025

Toni Maguire and Marc Clegg have asserted their moral right to be identified as the authors of this Work in accordance with the Copyright, Designs and Patents Act 1988.

For each paperback book sold, Bonnier Books UK shall donate 2.5% of its net receipts to the NSPCC (registered charity numbers 216401 and SC037717).

The authors of this work want to show Marc Clegg's experience growing up and so you will find language in this book which may be offensive. It is used to show the reality of the author's experience and they and the Publisher would like to add a trigger warning for that here.

This book is a work of non-fiction, based on the life, experiences and recollections of Marc Clegg. Certain details in this story, including names and locations, have been changed to protect the identity and privacy of the authors, their family and those mentioned.

Every reasonable effort has been made to trace copyright holders of material reproduced in this book, but if any have been inadvertently overlooked the publishers would be glad to hear from them.

www.bonnierbooks.co.uk

Contents

Prologue	1
1	8
2	20
3	28
4	30
5	33
6	43
7	50
8	53
9	55
10	69
11	83
12	89
13	94
14	97
15	99
16	110

17	*111*
18	*127*
19	*133*
20	*138*
21	*142*
22	*152*
23	*157*
24	*168*
25	*174*
26	*178*
27	*187*
28	*189*
29	*195*
30	*198*
31	*203*
32	*208*
33	*212*
34	*215*
35	*219*
36	*230*
37	*235*
38	*240*
39	*247*
40	*255*
Epilogue	*259*

Prologue

I was aged somewhere between 10 and 11 when curiosity caused me to search a cupboard that I soon found to be used for hiding secrets. Secrets that my mother most definitely didn't want me to know about. She couldn't have noticed that I watched her furtively putting envelopes inside and quickly closing its small door. It was this behaviour that made me want to know what was up there and I'll admit that, once the question entered my head, I couldn't stop wanting to know what it was that needed to be hidden from me. I was quite a nosey boy at that age and each time I saw Mum checking what I was doing and then, once satisfied that I was caught up in a book or something like that, she would stretch up and open that top door. But I couldn't help watching her out of the corner of my eye. I became even more curious when I saw some stiff papers and very large envelopes being placed up there.

One day when I was the only person in the house, I didn't hesitate to drag a chair underneath the cupboard and then, hoping no one would come back sooner than expected, I stood on it and reached out. It took just a few seconds for my fingers to grasp the knob and tug the door open. Rustling through the pile of papers, I discovered two that had my name on them. To begin with, I felt quite excited when I realised that I was holding my own birth certificate. That feeling disappeared the moment I saw there was a name I didn't recognise in the space for my father's name. Why wasn't Steve mentioned? I just hoped that some of the other documents in there might explain. But it didn't take long for me to realise that Steve, who I had always called Dad, was not my real father. Not only had he adopted me after he married Mum, but he had changed my original surname to his.

So, who was this man officially listed as my father? I kept picking up the pieces of paper because I wanted to know the answer but found nothing. My hands were now shaking, and in retrospect, I think that I was probably in a state of shock. Quickly and quietly, I put everything back as I had found it and hopped down off the chair, still none the wiser and unsure of what to do next.

It was later that day, my head still spinning, when I realised that I had never met anyone with the name shown on that certificate. If my real father had parents, then surely that meant I must have another set of grandparents. So where was he and why didn't I know him? Was it because he didn't like me? My overriding memory of that day is that I began to wish that I hadn't poked around at all. What I had learned was just too much for my younger self to handle. I suppose, at that age, curiosity made me want to find answers to the questions in my head, but a few days later, when I found out more, I realised just how dangerous my poking around had been. Not knowing that at the time, though, I kept telling myself that there must be more papers in the cupboard that would explain everything but I had to wait quite a while until I was on my own again.

It was a Saturday when my parents had gone out to take my younger brother and sister to visit a friend for a play date. They often did that and left me at home alone – I was used to it, and today, I was even grateful for it. I waited a few minutes in case they came back to pick up something they'd left behind and then did the same as before, dragging the chair to the secret cupboard.

Keep your ears open, my inner voice told me. *Can't have 'Dad' walking in and seeing you up there. Don't you know the trouble that would cause?* That thought certainly kept me alert while shuffling through the mass of papers. Most of them were not in the least bit interesting, but then I found one that nearly made me fall off the chair. After a few minutes, I discovered another certificate, which told me facts that, for a boy of my age, were extremely painful. Here, it was stated that the man who was my real father was only 22 when he died. The cause of death was suicide and, from the date, I worked out that I had been barely a toddler at the time.

All I wanted was to get down from that chair and forget everything that I had learned. My hands were shaking as I brushed a tear from my eye. First, I had found out that the man that I had always thought of as my dad wasn't my real dad after all and then I had learned that I would never get the chance to meet him. *Just look at some more, Marc, and you might find out why that happened*, my inner voice urged. The third useful document was Mum and Steve's marriage certificate. The date on it confirmed that they had married when I was two years old, only a year after my real father had died. I quickly shoved the document back in the cupboard. Their marriage had been in a registry office in Barnsley, South Yorkshire, but I was too young to have any memories of it. I suddenly realised that I'd never seen any photos from their wedding, certainly none were on display, nor could I find any of my real father. After ensuring that everything was back in its place, I finally climbed down, though now I was more determined than ever to find out why I had never been told who my real father was or what had happened to him.

I realised then how little I knew about my mum and the man I called 'Dad'. I wondered how long after their marriage they'd moved to Kexbrough, which was a village, not a huge town like Barnsley. I guessed that there must have been people who didn't approve of their marriage so soon after my father had died. Maybe that was the reason that I had never met my father's family. I'd always wondered.

I wish I had known that Steve was not my biological father. Having been made to believe he was made me feel quite angry, though once it had all sunk in, I began to feel pleased that he wasn't. I hated the idea that I might end up being like him. He was a man who could be charming, but that was only one side of him. People who knew him from the local pubs had no idea about his other side. Mum and I knew all about that, though. He had a temper that turned his fists into weapons that lashed out at Mum as well as me. I saw him as a frightening bully and couldn't understand why she still appeared to love him. As I got down from that cupboard and put the chair back in its place, I felt almost relieved that I wasn't Steve's son.

Luckily for me, I was able to settle back into reading my book before my mum came home. I wanted her to still believe that the cupboard was too high for me to see into. She was wrong not to have told me, but this was my secret and I didn't want to share it with her yet. Obviously, I wanted answers to all those questions still running through my head but, at this stage, I couldn't bring myself to ask her about what I had found out. I wondered if she would ever let me know who my real father was. Later, I would come to realise that Mum kept her secrets like dust motes, hanging in the air. She was never going to wipe them from her mind, nor did she want her children to know everything. I knew that if I had asked questions about what I had read on my birth certificate, she would have been disappointed in me, as well as very angry.

At least I don't have any of Steve's genes, I told myself as I did my best to act as nonchalantly as possible, having just had a lesson on genetics in biology class. I have to admit that my stepfather wasn't ill-tempered all the time. When he was in a good mood, he could make us all laugh, but his bad moods outweighed the good and they scared me.

It was after one of these dark moods a few days later, when his fist had landed on my shoulder and left a huge purple bruise, that I made up my mind to find out as much as I could about my real father. One of my uncles was always friendly to me and, being a similar age to Mum, he must have known my father. I was pretty certain he would be the one who could answer at least some of my questions, though I think he must have agreed never to mention him when I was there. Maybe Mum had told him not to say anything. The thought of her doing this made me feel a bit sick. Being only ten, I couldn't understand why Mum wanted my father to be forgotten. No doubt Steve did as well, or maybe it was he who insisted on it. That wouldn't have surprised me.

I still planned to go and see my uncle, but it took me a few days to pluck up the courage, given the questions I wanted to put to him. That was not the only reason I had to feel brave. Something inside my head was telling me, *Have another look in that cupboard. There's something you missed*, and so I needed to do that before I saw him.

I waited until Mum went out shopping the next weekend. As usual, Steve was in the social club with his mates watching the match and I just hoped he didn't rush home for any reason. My job was to keep an eye on my half-siblings so I put the TV on for them to watch cartoons. One more climb and I found the death certificate again. What did suicide mean? It was an illness that I hadn't heard of before. *It must be bad as it killed him*, I thought. I wanted to know exactly what it was, which made me climb down and get Mum's dictionary from the bookcase. I'm pretty sure that I froze with shock when I looked the word up. It did make some sense to me, though, as I couldn't understand why a 22-year-old would have died of something I hadn't known about. Why had he made the decision to leave this world? It was a question that kept running through my head, a question that made me feel even worse. Was there something about me that had caused it? There had to be a reason why I had never heard one word about him. That meant that all Mum's friends and relatives must have been made to promise never to say anything about him when I was around.

I went back to that cupboard and took the death certificate out. Folding it carefully, I put it in my pocket. At the back of my mind, I wanted to have it with me so my uncle couldn't say he didn't know what I was talking about. With the messy pile of papers and tatty old envelopes up there, hopefully Mum would never know what I'd been up, especially once I had managed to put it all back.

1

That weekend, I told my mum that I wanted to go and play with my cousins, which was a pretty regular occurrence as they lived within a ten-minute walk of our house. As I walked over to my Uncle Sam's house under a grey sky, all I kept thinking was, why had my father killed himself? I was nervous about asking the question, though, so I crossed my fingers in the hope that my uncle would not be annoyed about what I had learned. If he was, then he might tell Mum or Steve and then they would know I had been poking around in their private papers and I would be in trouble. I so hoped that my uncle wouldn't tell them but that didn't stop me. Even though it was a bit of a risk, I was determined to find out what had happened.

I felt slightly relieved when my uncle opened the door, rather than my aunt or one of my cousins. There he was with a beaming smile. 'Hello, young Marc, come on in! You want your cousins. They're out in the back garden if you want to walk through.'

Oh heck, what do I say now? I wondered. *Best explain,* I thought quickly.

I noticed his eyebrows raise a little when I said, 'I've got some things I want to ask you, if you don't mind? I think you might know the answers.'

No doubt when he said, 'Well, Marc, come in the sitting room with me,' he must have thought they were something to do with my homework or something like that. Still smiling, he led me in and told me to sit down on the settee while he sat on a chair near the fireplace. I could hear the excited shrieks of my cousins playing outside.

'What is it you want to ask, Marc?'

I took a deep breath and clenched my fists nervously as I tried to formulate the question about Mum having been married before. After a slight pause, a torrent of questions whirling around for days in my head came flying out of my mouth. I could tell then that my uncle was shocked and he was even looking a little worried. He must have wondered how I came to learn all these facts and he would have known how upset my mother would be if it all came out.

Silence hung in the room for a few seconds, but I just couldn't wait.

'I want you to tell me about my real dad,' I stammered out.

As our eyes met, the expression in his told me that this was not something he wanted to talk about.

'Uncle Sam, I've only just found out that Steve's not my real father. He had my surname changed to his after he and Mum were married, about a year after my dad died,' I told him.

There was a pause.

'How did you find all of this out, Marc?'

'I found some papers that told me all about my real father,' I said, pulling the death certificate out of my pocket and handing it to him.

'I see,' he murmured, looking down at it.

'I had to look up "suicide" in Mum's dictionary. First, I thought it must be an illness I had never heard of, but then I read the meaning – it made me feel awful.'

'I'm not going to ask you how you found that piece of paper. From what you've been telling me, I think you must have read more than this.'

I could tell that my uncle was thinking just how much he could let me know about my parents. I'm sure he didn't want me to get any more upset but I doubt he wanted me to ask Mum about my real father either.

'Did you know my dad well?' I asked.

'All right, Marc. Yes, of course I knew him, so I can tell you a few things about him but I want you to promise me that you won't say a word about this to your mother. She had planned to tell you about him when you were a little older and she wouldn't want you to know all this now.'

'OK, I promise that I won't say anything to Mum. I know it would upset her. That's why I came here to ask you about him.'

'OK, in that case, yes, he and I were friends. I can remember when your mother introduced him to us. I liked him straight away. Remember, they were both very young then and it was only a couple of weeks later that they told us all that they had got engaged. We hoped they would wait a while before they got married, but they refused. They had just turned twenty when your mother became pregnant with you.'

'Were they still together then?' I asked.

'They were but, sadly, they separated not long after you were born.'

At this, I reeled before asking, 'Why did they break up when I'd only just been born? Was it because of me?'

I could tell that my uncle didn't want to explain exactly how that had happened.

'Was it because he kept hitting her?' I persisted.

I'd seen Steve do this so often to Mum that it made me wonder if other men did the same to their partners.

'Good heavens, no! He wasn't that type of man at all,' my uncle insisted. 'Whatever made you think that?'

I could see the anger in his eyes when he said this and I think he knew just why I'd asked. I think he wished he hadn't asked me this because he must have heard all about Steve's bad temper. Still, I managed to avoid his questioning gaze, replying, 'Oh, I don't know ... Maybe something I saw on TV. So, was it Mum who left him, or was he the one who did?'

'It was your mother. She had her reasons.'

'What were they?'

I could tell then that he was desperately trying to think what he could say to me, his young nephew, so that I couldn't blame Mum for the depression that had caused my father to die. After a few seconds, he just told me that my father had made a stupid mistake.

'What was that?'

'He had an affair – do you understand what that means?'

I had to think about this for a moment before saying confidently, 'It means a married man who hasn't taken his wife out, but has gone with another woman.'

I had learned everything I knew about relationships from TV.

'That's right,' he said, no doubt relieved that at my age I didn't seem to know the details of what happened in an affair. 'Now, your mum didn't know about that for quite a while. It was after you were born that she found out about it. As far as I know, when she was pregnant with you, she put up with him going out with his mates. She never thought for one moment that it was a woman he was seeing.'

'So, how did she find that out?'

'It was a friend of your mother's who told her. I wish it was your father she had gone to first instead of telling your mum. He would have broken up with the girl as soon as he knew that her friend had found out about it, I'm sure. As you were only a few weeks old and your mum was feeling bad about all the weight she had gained and was exhausted the whole time, it wasn't the greatest moment to tell her.'

'So, how come she believed the friend? I mean, she must have hoped it was a lie. And how did the friend know that?'

At this my uncle smiled at me again before telling me, 'Your mum has never told me what she did to find out it was true. But knowing her, she probably found the girl and asked her a few questions. At least that's all I can think and I do remember that she was completely shattered when she found out that it was true. Despite this, she made her decision as soon as she was convinced about what he had been up to. You see, back then, she was a little different to now. In those days, she was a strong, decisive young woman and feisty too. She told me she was determined to stay firm. Your dad was devastated. Now I'm not saying what he did was right, not at all, but he was pretty broken by it. But he was a bit … much. I just hoped that he would stop annoying her. If he'd left her alone for a bit, I thought there might be a chance that she would take him back.'

I wish she had, then I wouldn't have Steve around, I thought to myself, but I didn't dare say this out loud.

My uncle must have seen how crestfallen I was because he added, 'One thing I want you to know, Marc, was the moment you came into this world, your dad really loved you. He came over to see me a few times when you and your mum were still in hospital. He kept telling me how happy he was about having a son and how he felt so delighted and proud when he was able to hold you for the first time – he had tears in his eyes.'

Hearing this, I was surprised to feel a tear trickling down my own cheek. I just wished that I could remember him.

'So, was he still seeing the other girl after I was born?' I managed to say because I didn't want him to stop telling me everything.

'As far as I know, he stopped seeing the girl then. But as I said, that was too late for your mother to forgive him and it was the worst time for her to have found out. She left him a few days after she had gone home with you, then moved in with your Aunt Mary.'

'Why was it the worst time for her when I had just been born?' I said, puzzled.

He laughed a little then. 'Come on, Marc, she loves you but you know how hard babies can be – there's always feeding, sleeping, naps. Your mum would have been up every few hours, every day. I'm sure you must have noticed that when your brother and sister arrived, how tired she was for more than just a few weeks?'

'I suppose so, but I didn't take much notice then. I remember she didn't have time to do much cooking for us,' I pondered.

'Well, then, she would have been the same when you were a baby.'

'You're right. I remember hearing Mum telling Steve that she was exhausted all the time and asking him to make the tea, but he's a terrible cook. Most nights, we had beans on toast – it was so boring!'

'I expect Steve tried to help her a little as he was older than your father.'

He never helps Mum at all, I thought to myself. *It was only because he wanted a meal, but I'd better keep quiet about him.*

'Why did my dad kill himself?' I finally managed to ask.

This was the saddest part of what I'd found out, along with how I couldn't remember him at all. Again, it brought tears to my eyes.

Uncle Sam passed me a tissue before saying, 'I can understand what you've been feeling, Marc. Just wait a minute or two and I'll explain a few more things to you. It was his brother Kevin who came over to tell me the sad news about your dad. It was a dreadful time. He was actually sitting where you are now and he told me a lot about your father's last days. He also gave me an envelope to give to your mum. I told him that I just couldn't give that to her, even though it was a letter your dad had written to her before he died.

'"She will need to read it," said Kevin. So, I promised him that I would take it to her. I know your dad should never have been unfaithful to her, but I still felt that, after you, his little boy, was born, they might have tried to get back together again. I dreaded telling her. I'd hoped your Aunt Mary would be there when I got to her house but she was out and that made it even worse. I knew that I had to tell her there and then so I took a deep breath and started as best I could. Then she opened the letter. That was enough to make her crumble. Of course, I stayed with you both until Mary arrived. When I walked back home, I was exhausted – you were so young. Your mum too. It was terrible.'

My uncle paused and I could see that he was also getting emotional. He went into the kitchen and came back with tea for himself and squash and chocolate biscuits for me before he continued, 'Now, I'm not excusing your father, but he'd never expected his fling would be found out. He must have been stupid and he was heartbroken when he read your mum's message that told him why she was leaving him. He was really shocked that she had taken you and just walked out of the house without saying a word. It was that note that finished him off, especially as he really loved you both. He came round to see me with tears in his eyes – or rather to ask me to speak to her. More than once he told me that he couldn't bear losing you. He wanted you and your mum to come back to him. He was nearly in tears again when he pleaded with me to persuade your mother to change her mind.

'So, what did you say?'

'I told him that I knew my sister very well and that the best thing he could do was to leave her alone for a while. Give her some time and she'd calm down. I knew she was still angry as well as feeling hurt about his affair. But he went back to the house more than once and that didn't go well, so I told him not to bother her there again – his knocking on the door was disturbing all the neighbours and he was waking you up after she'd spent hours getting you off to sleep.'

'Did he come over because he wanted to see me as well?' I asked eagerly.

'Yes, of course he wanted to do that. Not being able to spend more time with you made him feel worse. That's why he began bringing presents for the two of you. At least she accepted them, but she never let him into the house, always kept him at the front door.

'Your mum told me she knew why he was being so

generous. To be fair, if you were awake, she always brought you to the door so that he could see how much you were growing each time. You were his son, after all, and he had a right to see you. I think she was just beginning to soften and feel sorry for him. She thought he needed to see you when he came over. He looked so miserable.'

'Did he hold me and give me cuddles?'

'Yes, your mum eventually allowed him to do that a few times – she trusted him.'

'So what happened after he kept visiting Mum and me?'

'She gave him certain times when he could visit and told him to stick to them, but one day, he'd had a few drinks and lost track of time. He turned up at the house when she was busy feeding you. She certainly didn't want him pounding on the door after she'd asked him not to. Your mum had no idea that this was the last time she was going to see him. She was so annoyed that she had to put you down and, of course, that was enough for a hungry baby to howl loudly, which you did! She was even more annoyed when she smelt that he'd been drinking on his way there so she asked him to leave, but he got himself into a state. He kept asking her to come back and, at the same time, he tried to push some presents into her hands. If only he hadn't been so drunk, as well as coming at the wrong time, she might have taken them. Instead, she told him that she didn't want them and slammed the door in his face. He wasn't in a good place but your mum had no idea just how bad it was. He must have apologised for his behaviour in the letter he wrote for her to read. I know that the memory of the last time she saw him has haunted her ever since.'

'So, how did he kill himself?' I forced myself to ask.

'Are you sure you want to know all this, Marc?' my uncle asked, looking at me softly.

'Yes, I really do, please,' I pleaded with him.

'OK, if you're really sure,' he said hesitantly. 'Well, I can try to offer some reassurance here because it wasn't too grisly. It's called carbon-monoxide poisoning, which is caused by breathing in a good deal of gas. It doesn't cause pain at all. In fact, it's a peaceful way to go if you have to go at all. It wouldn't have taken long for him to fall asleep and then, after a while, he wouldn't have woken up.

'It was your Uncle Kevin who found him several hours later. I don't know how he coped, finding his younger brother dead like that.'

'But why did he do it? I mean he was only twenty-two and he would have had lots of years left. Then he and I would have known each other and I would have had a father I loved and who loved me?' I stuttered.

The tears started to fall and the depth of my sadness was laid bare. More tears slid down my face and, seeing them, my uncle came and sat next to me and put his arms around me. He looked just as sad as I was feeling.

'Now I know it's really difficult for you to have discovered all this and maybe now you can understand why your mum didn't want you to know about it until you were much older. That's the reason for her not saying anything about him.'

'But why did he have to go?' I persisted.

'He had very bad depression – he had always suffered from it anyway but his affair just made it worse. He thought he had done something terrible and that he wasn't a good person. The letter he had left for your mum made her cry a lot. She was inconsolable and had to lie down after she read it. I tried my best to comfort her. When she finally managed to sit up again, she handed it to me. In it he had written that he was sorry for what he had done. The last sentence was him telling her that he had made up his mind to go but that he still loved you both. I think those words have never left her mind.'

Hearing this made me feel a little better. I then asked my uncle what my father had looked like.

'I have a photo of him,' he told me. He got up and went over to the bookshelf, where he brought down a box and took it out to show me.

I was nervous to finally see my dad after imagining him for so long and I could hardly believe how nice he looked when I saw that picture. He was really good-looking and he looked so young and happy – I could just tell that he would have been a much better father to me than my 'dad' Steve. He had a kind smile and I didn't think for one moment that he would have lashed out at me with his fists.

'One more thing ... Why was I called Marc with a "c" and not a "k"? The school always gets it wrong!'

'Haha! Your parents loved the band T. Rex so they named you after the lead singer, Marc Bolan.'

That made me smile a little.

2

A couple of days later, I saw my cousin Jim. He was three years older than me and I always found him great fun. We walked down to the River Dearne and sat watching the creamy white ducks with their little yellow ducklings paddling by their sides. It was while there that I couldn't help telling him that I now knew Steve was not my father.

'You knew that too, didn't you?' I countered.

'OK, yes, my dad told me, but how did you find out, Marc? Was it your mum who said? I thought she was going to wait until you were a bit older.'

'No, it wasn't her. I found it out from some papers in a cupboard, but she doesn't know that I know. Best not let her find out. I know it would just upset her, especially if she thinks I was snooping behind her back.'

I didn't say anything about the conversation with my uncle. I had promised not to mention what he had told me and I was determined to stick to that promise.

'We all knew, but Dad said we shouldn't say anything because your mum wanted to tell you what happened to your real dad,' Jim told me.

I just smiled then and said, 'I thought so.'

'By the way, there's something else that might amuse you – it's about Steve. My mum and dad say he's "conceited". I'm not exactly sure what that means but it's one of the words they use about him. Though there's others, especially when they say what a bully he is. I know what that means. They really don't like him at all. We all love your mum, though. I overheard my dad saying he wished she had chosen a kinder man to be with instead of him. I know he can be aggressive too. I've heard that he had a bit of a reputation long before your mum married him. Goodness knows why she did. My mum said she thinks it was just because your mum was so devastated about your real dad's death. She was really broken.

'But my mum said she shouldn't have let us overhear what she'd been saying – I know she was pretty angry when she knew we'd heard. Auntie Mary and Mum got us to promise that we wouldn't talk about that to you or anyone outside of our family as well.

'I know about your dad's funeral, though …'

At this, my eyes widened in disbelief. I couldn't believe they all knew about this and they'd talked about it behind my back.

'My parents and Auntie Anne, who had also been fond of your father, went to the funeral with your mum. I expect they were prepared for your dad's family to ignore them –

they thought they would blame her for what happened. I know they didn't sit near them but stayed on the other side of the church.'

He looked at me and saw tears falling.

'Marc, don't cry, please. Maybe I shouldn't have told you this stuff.'

'But I want to know,' I protested. 'I can't ask Mum. I don't want her getting upset. Do you know any more about the funeral? I know you would have been told about it. I just want to know as much as I can.'

'All right then, I'll try and tell you. But I didn't go. I was too young, so it's just what I've heard. Mostly about the speeches and the nice things people said about your dad. His brother Kevin did a speech. Mum told me they were all so upset that they couldn't remember what it was he said, although it was really nice things about his brother. I remember my mum saying your mum's legs nearly gave way when your dad was actually buried. Mum and Auntie Mary managed to hold her up and helped her walk to their car. They knew she needed looking after for a while, which was why they took her back to their house.'

'So where were you when your parents were at the funeral, and where was I?'

'We were both with a babysitter. It was Hazel. Do you remember her? She got married a couple of years ago. Though I was only about three then. I can't remember what you were like or the day itself. It's just all the gossip about the past I hear from Mum and her sisters that tells me what happened on that day. I did overhear my mum say that she and Auntie Mary thought that, since your dad had died in the way he did, your mum didn't seem to have much strength or fight left. Mum had her staying for a couple of days so that she could help her get herself together before she went home.'

'When did she meet Steve then, do you know?' I asked.

'No, not really, but from what I've heard, it was only a few months after the funeral.'

'So how did she meet him?'

'I haven't a clue,' Jim admitted, 'but I guess he might have had some friends that your mum also knew. Maybe she met him in one of their houses. I expect he heard about your dad's funeral. What your mum wouldn't have known was that that, once he got her to marry him, she was never allowed to talk about her first husband. Pretty bad, don't you think? But it makes sense now that you didn't have a clue.'

'Yes, I would have wanted to know about him ages ago.'

Jim looked around almost sheepishly before continuing.

'Marc, have you ever heard what Steve did once they were married?'

'Did they have a honeymoon?'

I thought everyone would have had one.

'I don't know, but that's not what I meant. Do you know what he did just a few days after they were married?'

'No, not really, but I think he did a lot of things then. Got Mum pregnant twice, didn't he? So just tell me what you mean.'

'He found her wedding album, which she had hidden in

her underwear drawer of all places. It had loads of photos of her and your dad. He got rid of it, maybe even burned it. It's a good thing she had a few other photos hidden elsewhere, my mum said. Your mum took them to her for safekeeping so that they could be kept for you when you're a bit older. She was worried that, if Steve found them, he would have got rid of them too.'

'I suppose there's none of those photos still in your house?' I asked hopefully. I was wishing, praying there were some others for me to see. Looking at pictures of my dad made me feel closer to him.

'I don't think my mum will let you see them. When she tells you about your dad, mine will let you look at them. You'll just have to wait a little.'

I did my best to stop his chatter about Mum's past. It was Steve I wanted to hear about; even though he'd been my dad for the last eight years, I didn't know that much about him. If only Mum had carried on being the same young woman my uncle had told me about, I don't think she would have stayed with Steve. That made me wish that, somewhere deep inside her, she was still brave enough to leave him. I voiced this to Jim.

'That's what my mother wishes too,' he said. 'We'd heard about those fists of his. "Nasty weapons," my mum says. I've heard her say that she thinks you both live in fear of him. That's true, isn't it?'

But I just stared at Jim and gulped. Even though it was true, I didn't want to talk about it.

'I try to keep out of his way as much as possible,' was all I managed to say. Fiercely loyal, I knew I had to stop myself from telling any of my relatives about the extent of Steve's bad temper. Nor would I mention the rows between him and Mum.

How come my cousin knew so much? Eavesdropping, I supposed.

'Your mum had purple bruises on her arms last week. I expect they were there in other places too. Her excuse was that she had tripped over the mat and that was all she would say. Of course, Mum didn't believe a word of it. I heard her telling Dad that she was worried because she knew it was Steve who had caused them.'

Now, as I had heard that particular row between them, I was fairly certain I knew those bruises had come from him – there were enough cries of pain and shouting. Considering that they went out together a lot, it would have been hard for other people to believe how much he controlled her. It was only Mum's family who were convinced there was violence involved.

I didn't respond to Jim as I didn't like to talk much about what happened in our home.

Seeing that I wasn't going to say anything, he came up with another question: 'I know a story about you and him when you were about two. Do you want to hear it?'

I really didn't but, knowing my cousin, I doubt if I could have stopped him, even though I had a feeling that this story of his would not be a good one. I also knew that I'd been the one to start the conversation, but now I was beginning to regret it. Foolishly, I found myself nodding and saying 'OK, go on then.'

That story about Steve was far worse than I thought. It certainly made me shiver.

'Well, maybe it's lucky that we can't remember,' Jim said with a grin, before telling me that, apparently, Steve was a bit jealous and didn't like me sitting on Mum's lap – 'It was your contented gurgles that drove him mad. Imagine being jealous of a baby! He wouldn't put up with it and seems he told her to put you down on the floor. Of course, she didn't, which made him really angry. Once she said that, he jumped up and grabbed hold of you by the shoulders so that he could take you off her lap. Crazy, right?'

'How do you know all this, Jim? You were only about five then,' I asked sceptically.

'It's a story I've heard my parents talking about. They've never forgotten it and it really made them worried about you, as well as your mum.'

'So, what happened next?'

'Apparently, he carried you over to the fireplace and dangled you just above the fire!'

'Bloody hell! Well, I haven't got any burns on my body so at least he didn't drop me in it,' I said optimistically.

'Pretty scary! My mum says he told your mum that he would keep lowering you down an inch at a time until she said she was sorry for having you on her lap. Can you believe it? I heard that he laughed at her. She told my mum that.

He seemed to think it was funny and started lowering you down a little more. Well, that was enough to make your mum scream when she saw him doing that, she was so scared he would get burns on your legs. She was hysterical by then.'

'Did I start crying as well?' I said, horrified.

'I'm not sure – probably, or maybe you thought it was a game? I doubt he'd have gone that far, even if he's a nasty bastard. My mum said he wanted her to be scared enough so that he would always be in control of her. Your mum was shaking with fear.'

'I'm not surprised and it's a good thing he didn't drop me,' I observed.

That story made me think that this must have been the beginning of Mum's nerves sapping away all her strength. It made me feel sad for her, that she also had to protect me like that. I remembered how my uncle had described Mum when she was young: strong, feisty even. How I wished that she had been able to stay being the woman who would have stood up to him, then and now.

3

I'll tell you what I think is so sickening about Steve and the thing that I couldn't shake off after hearing Jim tell that story: it's to use a toddler as a tool to threaten and control. It's pretty sick and shows you just what kind of a person he was. My mum must have been really scared, of him and what he might do to me. Whatever it was Steve wanted Mum to do, she began to feel wary of him the whole time. Talk about playing games. I remember even as a young boy that he used to say that her nerves were not good at all during her two pregnancies, but it was more likely that he had caused this.

'Your mum broke down one evening when I was in the sitting room with my mum and dad,' Jim told me. 'She blurted out a lot before Mum had a chance to ask me to leave, so I heard what was happening between her and Steve at that time. As I said, my parents have always been worried about her. I know they're concerned about you too – I hear them talking a lot.

'They say he bullies you because you're not his son. At least that's what I heard. Dad's right, isn't he?'

'He can be very strict,' was all I could muster.

'Oh, come on, Marc.'

But I just shrugged and told him I'd had enough and I wanted to go home.

4

All these years later, I still have memories of my childhood that come flooding back into my dreams. Within seconds, they turn into gristly nightmares. Even now, I can hear Mum's screams in my head after the sound of Steve's fist thumping on her body. When that nightmare comes, I somehow manage to open my eyes and make those pictures of my past go away. Even now, I still don't believe that those dreams will ever leave me.

There are so many memories I want to forget, but much as I have tried, I can't push them away. Steve's anger towards me – which I now know began when I was very young – has stayed with me over the years, though there was one time, when I was about 11 years old, when he showed a rare streak of kindness towards me that I hold onto in my darkest moments.

When one of those dreams has disturbed me, I tend to get some photos out of the drawer near my bed. They are the ones

I have of when I was really small, the ones where I looked so happy. They are the ones I enjoy looking at, for they tell me that there were good times for my younger self. Which, of course, made Mum take the photos. They make me think of happier days and, of course, there were some of those.

There's one picture that I love looking at. It was taken on the morning of my first day at school. Mum took the photo of me when I was dressed in my short grey trousers and my dark navy blazer. In my right hand was a bag to hold my crayons and pencils. On my face was a wide, happy smile. After that photo was taken, she took hold of my hand and we walked together to the school.

I found out fairly soon just what a lovely time this was for her and for me, and how she'd spent time that summer teaching me the alphabet as well as my times tables. I can actually remember that first day at school well and particularly when we got to the school gates. I met some of my classmates for the first time and Mum met some of the other mums. There was one who introduced herself to Mum and her son Rob to me. It was he who, within a few days at school, became my best friend and we are still friends to this day. We find it extraordinary that our friendship has lasted for all these years after everything we've been through. It's our mothers who remember what we were like then and they can't help telling us little stories from our pasts.

I've got other photos of me from that time that were taken every year on the first day of the new school year, and with Rob too. I love the ones when we went into senior school together. When we were little, we were nearly always in the playground together, and after a few weeks, we were going to each other's homes. When Rob's mum asked if she could bring me back for tea when school finished, it was also the beginning of Mum often doing the same and a new, special friendship was formed that was so important for both of us and gave us a special connection that helped us through so many hard times.

5

Mum was really pleased that I was enjoying school, especially as I'd quickly made such a good friend in Rob. Jane, Rob's mother, was also great and I loved going to their home after school or at the weekends. She always made such a fuss of me and seemed to enjoy seeing us going out into the garden to play.

As time went by and we'd been at school for a few years, our mothers stopped coming to collect us, confident that we were now able to walk back to our homes so long as we went together. This was the nineties after all – things were considered safer back then, even if you can't imagine this happening now. I would often go to Rob's house or he came to mine. His mum began inviting me to go over at weekends and sometimes I would stay overnight. Excitedly, I would pack pyjamas and things for the morning in my tiny blue case. I loved staying there as Rob's parents were always so nice to me and his mum cooked really tasty food. Although we had both been making other friends during our school years, Rob and I remained very close friends.

It took about two years of being in school for me not to want to go home straight away when the classes were finished. Apart from the afternoons when I knew I was going to Rob's house, I hated the sound of the bell ringing that told us we could leave for the day. That sound got all my friends leaping up and pushing everything into their schoolbags as fast as possible before they rushed out the door. Each time I had to go straight home, the ever-present question came into my head: would Steve be there with his bad temper, antagonised even further by the sight of me, or would it just be Mum, waiting for me with a broad smile?

That uncertainty encouraged me to linger on the school's grounds for a bit longer. I'd chatter away to my fellow pupils as I walked with them to the gates. I did my best to say just about anything I could think of to get their attention – I could act as though I was a boy who was able to tell stories and make jokes that made them laugh. That pleased me; I never wanted the boys in my class to guess the real reason I liked hanging back to talk to them. I certainly didn't want the other kids to know about my problems at home. That would have made me look pathetic and then they would feel sorry for me, and I certainly didn't want that.

There were days at school when I couldn't push away the pictures in my head of Steve, his face distorted by anger. Quite often, something he thought about or heard on the television was enough to make him flare up. Apart from loathing his bullying tone, it bothered me when I had to try to do my homework in this atmosphere and it was becoming increasingly difficult as the years went by. It was not easy to concentrate with his angry voice in the background. Often, I had to use a torch and complete my tasks after I had gone to bed. I knew if Mum had seen my light on, she'd tell me off for not finishing my homework earlier, rather than appreciate just why that was. The torch was a better option for me.

There were so many afternoons when I wished I could find another place to work because Steve's grumbling and shouting at Mum upset us both, as well as making concentration a problem for me. As I dawdled home, I just hoped he and Mum weren't going to have another nasty row. My worrying about the atmosphere in our house often stopped me going to sleep straight away. *You're in your last year at junior school*, my inner voice kept telling me. *Your homework is important, isn't it? Don't let the hard work you've put in over the last five years just slip away.* So I made myself go back in time and think of all the topics I had studied in school from when I started.

As I neared the end of junior school, I really enjoyed reading and my maths was strong. Mum had helped me a lot in the early years when I struggled to grasp how to multiply numbers. As the volume of homework increased, I thrived, getting good grades. If I did well, it would impact which class I would be placed in at senior school. I wanted to be in the top set, as did Rob.

When I was leaving for school one morning, Mum told me that Steve would be home early. He was a miner – it ran in his family – and he had an evening meeting with some other local miners later on and needed to prepare. Evidently, this was because there was trouble in most of the mines in Yorkshire at this time in the 1980s. Not that I had any idea at my young age what the reason was and, frankly, I wasn't that interested. If my stepdad was out when I got home, it really suited me. So, what bothered me was not what was happening to the mines, but that he would be home when I first got there. Hopefully, he would be tied up and that would preoccupy him, and he would just leave me alone.

I can understand now why I was nervous. I wanted my schoolwork to be as perfect as I could make it – I suppose even at that time I thought, by achieving good grades, I could make something of my life and get out of the situation I was living in sooner rather than later. But as I've said, when Steve was at home, he often broke my concentration, especially as his temper would flare up over very little. Whatever was in his head, it got him shouting at both Mum and me. I couldn't understand why he seemed so angry with us when, as far as I knew, we hadn't done anything wrong. And it was always aimed at me, or Mum, never my brother or sister. He always made me feel left out.

His bullying made working on the kitchen table almost impossible but, in our small home there was nowhere else I could do it. It was not easy to concentrate on an essay when there was shouting around me, distracting me. As I've said, I often had to wait until I was in bed and then I would finish my homework up there. How I hated witnessing the aggression Steve aimed at my mum. That made me wish that I could be somewhere – anywhere – else. And although I tried to cut the noise out, I couldn't help but want to be there to witness it all, maybe in case things got too bad because I always feared that happening.

What I was unaware of at the time was that Steve knew that there were going to be bigger problems in the mines where he worked in the north of England. He must have been hoping that he'd got it wrong, but he hadn't. That was enough to keep him worried as well as ill-tempered. His behaviour became worse and worse.

That summer, just before I started at senior school, I began to enjoy reading more and more. I would go to the library and take out a few books that went straight onto my bedside table. Back then, I was hooked on Judy Blume, Virginia Andrews, Stephen King and James Herbert. That was another reason I kept my torch in my drawer. When lights had to go out, I would continue reading in secret. It was my escape.

I tried to find more reasons to be out of the house and, as I loved singing, I joined the church choir for a while. Choir practice was on a Wednesday evening and there were services to attend on Sundays. Another reason for staying out of the way of Steve – besides, I really enjoyed it. But I couldn't keep out of the house all day. I truly believed that life without him would make both me and my mum happier; it would definitely make my life better. Not that my siblings felt that way. I could see that they loved him, especially my sister, who clung to him whenever he was home. How could a man be so different with his children? The answer was I wasn't his.

Images of my younger self keep flooding into my head from that time. I can see the troubled boy I was then; a boy who didn't have any idea how much his life was going to change, and not for the better either.

Within a year, the mines would be closed and many families in our area would be affected. Steve must have felt that it was coming. I can vaguely remember him talking about the mines to Mum, but I didn't take much notice at the time. Like his father, he had gone to work in the mines as soon as he left school. Now he had advanced to a fairly high position in the union. All I knew about mines then was that men mainly worked underground and sometimes there were accidents.

Kexbrough might have been small but it was still a good place to live when I was young. It was almost like being part of a big family. The miners' families were all so friendly. Almost every time I went out, people I knew would greet me with big smiles and warm hellos. If Mum was with me, conversations would begin between them all. Although Steve kept talking about problems coming, none of the women Mum met ever said anything about being worried about their husbands' jobs. It was more talk about summer holidays and nights out at the club that interested them. Hardly surprising as everyone looked forward to their time off, particularly the summer holidays, the biggest holiday of the year. Groups of families visited camping sites in the south of England and

Unloved 39

some even had plans to fly over to southern Spain. After all, food and drink was cheaper there, they told us, and the weather was more reliable than in the north of England.

There was one evening when we were all sitting together after tea when Steve, having had a few cans of beer, began to tell us stories about his earlier days working in the mines. He had been working in Barnsley for well over ten years by then. The first part of a story he told us happened not long after he had left school, when he, like many other boys, had followed his father down the mine he worked in. Those tales of his early years in the mines sounded so amusing that he even had us laughing. The last one he told us was about the closure of the northern mines, which wrecked the lives of so many families. There were huge strikes and the government brought up police from other areas; there were fights, many men and even women supporting the miners were arrested, but the strikes continued. There was a slogan coined then which so many people chanted out loud when the police were there to try and stop the strike: 'Close a pit, kill a community'. Those were the words that flew in the faces of the police. Sadly, that slogan turned out to be the truth for so many of the families.

Steve then told us how, in Barnsley, most men were in full employment, as were some of the women, who worked in the offices. The men worked hard so that they were well-off and they were more than just contented as they and their families enjoyed life.

Steve had brought some photos down to show us the huge

Club Ba-ba that was in Barnsley during the early seventies. 'That club was really famous,' he said.

'It looks like a stunning place,' I agreed, for once engaged with what my stepfather had to say.

'It was, Marc,' he conceded, 'and ten years ago, it was full of happy people. A happiness that ended almost overnight.'

Steve went on to tell us how the miners' girlfriends and wives loved to dress up on the nights they visited the club. On the weekend, the place was full as the miners were paid on Fridays. The wages they earned then were enough for them to enjoy a great night out without having to budget too much. Those with small children paid for babysitters and, although teenage kids could go with them, those that weren't interested in the bands volunteered their babysitting services instead. But most teenagers simply loved the band – The Grumbleweeds – with their jokes between singing sets. From what Steve told us, there was a popular mix of cabaret singers as well as comedians and dancers. The magician Paul Daniels was one entertainer and Gerry Marston and Tony Christie were among the well-known singers who were often on Ba-ba's stage.

'Everyone loved them,' Steve sighed and Mum nodded in agreement.

He then showed us other photos of some very pretty girls wearing sparkling mini-dresses. We could see they were dancing on the stage in front of the band.

'The single guys really fancied them,' Steve said. 'That club was miles better than the one we have in Kexbrough.'

Unloved 41

'What else did Ba-ba's have?' I asked curiously.

'There was also a casino there. People played cards such as blackjack, poker, and sometimes even roulette. And they had a great fancy dining room as well. Those meals were amazing and so were the bottles of wine that just about everyone ordered.'

'What happened to the club?' I wanted to know.

Steve told us that, because some of the mines had been closed, a lot of the miners had become unemployed. Some of them had moved to different towns to try to get some employment.

'Unfortunately, a few of the men on the strikes went too far, chucking stones and bricks at the police, and some even ended up in prison.'

Not that Steve blamed them; tempers were high. 'The police did for them, though, and many of them went inside for GBH and rioting. Sadly, so many of the older men never found jobs again and, without them, the club had no choice but to close down.'

Steve then told us a bit about the families who went from reasonable levels of income to poverty. It was so swift, some could scarcely take it in: 'I had so many friends then who were completely devastated. I didn't know what I could do to help them. I was one of the men who was on the strikes then. We were all so angry about how shoddily the men were being treated. The miners fought to prevent their pits from being closed. The government wanted the pits closed and they often used the London police to put pressure on the miners.'

Steve was convinced that it would all start up again in the mining towns in our area. He had witnessed the heart going out of a place before as jobs went, men became unemployed and the women working in the offices were also let go. Because they were broke, men had to go elsewhere to try to find employment and that was no good for their families, especially the boys.

I knew that already – I had seen what happens to boys when their fathers leave.

6

Whatever sad stories I heard and excuses I was given about Steve's concern for the future of the men who worked under him, they didn't encourage me to forgive him for his behaviour. Hadn't I seen him hit my mother more than once? There were such violent rows in our home that I would never forget. I remember coming in from school one day and seeing Steve's face red with anger. One look at Mum and I could tell she had been crying but, at the age I was then, there was nothing I could do.

'Take your homework straight upstairs, Marc,' she whispered to me one night as soon as I walked in the door. I knew she meant it would be safer for me to be out of the way. I had heard their shouting as I walked up the path. From the pleading look she gave me, I knew she wanted me to be out of Steve's way in case he turned on me. I rushed up the stairs with my satchel and stayed in my room until I thought it was safe again downstairs. But the shouting didn't stop and, although I tried to concentrate on my English essay, I felt sick, hairs prickling at the back of my neck. I was really frightened about what might be happening down there.

It was about half an hour later when I heard the door slamming shut and the house seemed to shake with its veracity. I hadn't realised until then that I was almost holding my breath all this time and I let it out, which made me relax a bit. I knew it must be him who had left. Mum wouldn't have gone out and left us kids. No doubt he would be on his way to the pub, where he would be quickly downing pints of beer, which would make his temper even worse. I just hoped that he would swallow enough to make him fall asleep in his chair as soon as he came back.

I went downstairs and there was Mum, both angry and upset, twisting a tissue in her fingers as she sat on the settee.

'I can't stand much more of this,' she said tearfully and I could see the beginning of bruises on her arms and neck. 'I've made a decision, darling,' she told me. 'We can talk about it in the morning. Steve has to go out very early.'

I can remember we had our tea together and my siblings, who had also crept up to their room, had to be coaxed down as they, too, were traumatised. After they were fed, Mum put them in front of the TV until it was time for them to go to bed. All she said to me after I had helped her clear the table was that she had taken them up to their room as soon as she saw a row brewing.

'They're too young to understand,' she explained.

I was in no mood to watch cartoons so I went to my room

but I was still agitated so I couldn't concentrate enough to do my homework. Instead, I pulled up one of my library books and laid down on my bed reading, keeping one ear open to see if Steve came home.

It was when I woke up in the morning and began to get ready for school that I noticed that there was no noise downstairs at all. For once, I couldn't hear anything, not even my brother and sister chattering. The silence made me feel a bit nervous so I was relieved to see Mum sitting at the kitchen table with a cup of tea.

'Did Steve go to his meeting early?'

'He did, thank goodness.'

I looked around the room but there was no sign of my siblings coming down. 'Where are they? Still upstairs?' I asked Mum.

'They're at your Auntie Jean's. I took them over once Steve had gone – he won't be back for ages. We're moving out while he's at work, but for now, we're going to stay with my friend Eve. I rang her and she's said we're all welcome to stay with her. Now, go and get what you need: your schoolbooks and your clothes. And best not forget the library books. We don't want to pick up fines.' She handed over a large holdall and I saw she had another one standing by the door already bursting with her clothes.

'I'll check your bedroom before we leave in case you've forgotten something. Just throw in as much as you can.'

That told me that we were not just spending a night with Eve, who, thankfully, I liked. Her house was large and comfortable. Her husband worked on the oil rigs so he was away from home a lot. When he was back, he was always friendly. Mum and I had enjoyed going there with my two siblings as well.

I began to feel that our life was going to be a happier one with Steve out of the picture, though I couldn't help but wonder if Mum was really going to take my younger brother and sister with us – and how would Steve react? Even though my siblings had heard the rows and seen Mum's bruises and must have known what caused them, they still loved their father. I wasn't really sure what my brother thought because we were never that close, but I knew that my sister thought the world of Steve. She was the one who would want to stay with him, not Mum and I. I think Mum knew that, and their lack of closeness made her a little sad. I wanted my siblings to come with us. I couldn't imagine leaving them behind.

'They don't seem to want to go,' Mum told me wearily when I asked her. 'If their dad is happy having them here with him, there's not much I can do about it. The last thing I want is for him to be looking for us and causing problems because I've taken those two with us so, for now, he can look after them. He'll soon see it's not easy.'

Steve would have created a lot of trouble – I'm sure he would have contacted the social services so they would come knocking on Eve's door. If my siblings were questioned, I was sure they would say they wanted to live with their daddy. Nor would either of them talk about the rows or the beatings. Mum looked so sad at the thought of leaving her children but

I think she knew the games that Steve had played, and he'd manipulated them, using them as a weapon against her.

'You know where Eve lives, don't you, Marc? When you leave school today, you can come straight over to her house.'

'I will, Mum,' I said, feeling a lot happier at the thought I would not have to see Steve that night. In fact, I hoped that we would be staying with her for a long time. I liked Eve, but most importantly, I knew Mum would be safe.

I wondered then what Steve would do about his children. Later, I found out that he didn't do much at all. He just hired a childminder who took them to school, picked them up and fed them their tea. Steve came home in time to put them to bed. Shame he wasn't like that when we all lived together.

A huge weight was lifted. When school finished that day, I made my way over to Eve's much faster than I did when I was going to our home. In fact, I was looking forward to seeing how my life would be in a new environment. Although I knew it was probably only temporary, and a lot still needed to be sorted out, at least it would be peaceful for a time.

During that first week at Eve's, I found myself feeling much less stressed and Mum seemed like a different person. She was not in the least bit uptight there and it was lovely to get home and hear the two women chatting and laughing when I walked in.

That first day, Mum got up and gave me a hug and Eve told me she had made a sandwich for me.

'Come in the kitchen,' she said, ruffling my hair. 'I thought you might be hungry after all last night's drama.'

I trotted in behind her and there on the table was a thick cheese sandwich and a glass of orange juice.

'You can do your homework in here. Have you got much?'

'Quite a lot, and I didn't finish everything last night, but I should get it all done in about an hour and a half.'

Come the evening, after we'd had our tea, I was able to watch television with Mum and Eve. Even that was different from when we were at home. Steve just sat in front of the TV and clicked on the remote to whatever he wanted to see, or watched something and got increasingly angry. He rarely asked Mum or me if there was something we wanted to watch. Eve, on the other hand, passed over the magazine with the TV listings in and we all decided together.

Over the first week, I could see that Mum's bruises had faded quite a lot and I felt that we were much safer at her friend's house. It pleased me that she seemed more cheerful as well and I realised I hadn't heard a raised voice for a whole seven days.

Another week went by, and I was feeling so comfortable there. I had the use of a small bedroom which looked out over the garden. I ate my meals with Mum and Eve, who always asked me a few questions about school and how I was getting on. I nearly told her how much easier it was for me to do my homework in her house.

'I like my school. I'm getting good marks for most of my subjects, which I'm really happy about, and my English has improved since I found out that I enjoy reading,' I said instead.

'Good for you, Marc! Reading is a great way to broaden

your general knowledge and your vocabulary too,' she said as she placed my tea in front of me.

Mum helped out with the cooking, and the food the pair of them prepared was really good. Almost like being in a restaurant, I thought. Eve had lots of recipe books and they would experiment together. I was seeing a different side to my mum and it was such a joy to see her so happy after such a long time. But, sadly, it wasn't to last long.

7

It must have been about three weeks after we had moved to Eve's that I came in from school to find Mum wasn't there. I asked Eve where she had gone, but she didn't seem to know. Or rather she did but she didn't want to tell me. All she said was that she thought Mum was meeting up with a friend, but I didn't believe it. I had a horrible feeling then that she was out seeing Steve and, sadly, my suspicion was to prove correct. To my horror, when she returned, she told me she had decided we were going back to our house, making some feeble excuses for Steve's behaviour.

'The thing is he's so worried about the strikes that might have to begin again soon. Strikes being organised by the leader of the miners' union, Arthur Scargill. It's that Margaret Thatcher. She wants to close the mines. Eve, he was there in the seventies when so much went wrong, so I can understand why he's so angry. Those strikes had awful results. That's why he's worried. He thinks this one will be just as bad.

So I can't blame him. He's just wound up ... Well, you would be, wouldn't you?'

'What's happened now, Mum?' I asked.

'I'll get Steve to explain it to you. It's a pity that it's the politicians who can make people stop being able to work for companies they've known for years, isn't it?'

Before I could ask what she meant, Mum told me that Steve was very sorry about upsetting us. 'He's apologised a lot and he asked me to tell you he's sorry about his shouting. He's promised me that he'll act differently when we go back and he'll be quiet so you can do your homework.'

I couldn't believe it – how Mum could forgive him so easily! I was more than disappointed at having no choice but to go back home. The summer holidays were going to start about a week later. The thought of being around the house a lot of the day with him there bothered me and so I decided to tell her.

'He won't be there much, son,' Mum insisted when I brought it up. 'He's one of the leaders in the mines and he's needed there a lot.' She smiled as she said this, which made me realise that she was actually happy to be going back to him. Maybe this was what she'd hoped for all along? I could see there was no point in trying to change her mind so I just acted as though I wasn't bothered.

Once we had packed to go, Eve told us she had really enjoyed having us both in her house.

'You'll come with your mum when I invite you both over for tea?' she asked.

Mum and I said we would love that and we thanked her for our stay. We had a cup of tea together and I managed to eat my sandwich, trying to act as normally as possible, then Eve rang for a taxi.

About 15 minutes later, Eve helped us carry our luggage outside to the waiting cab. I waved to her, feeling so disappointed in Mum that I could hardly make myself talk on the short journey home.

It was Steve who, with a wide smile on his face, opened the front door and picked up our cases. My little brother and sister were so pleased to see us that they came running over and Mum and I bent down to give them hugs.

When I looked up, I could see Steve smiling indulgently. I was surprised to see that the smile took in both of us.

Perhaps he had changed.

But life as I knew it would never be the same again.

8

Kexbrough was a small South Yorkshire mining town and there, many years before, a club for the miners and their families was built. My parents and their friends went there often. They went to drink and socialise, play darts and pool, and their children all knew each other.

In the larger towns not far from us, parents wanted to keep an eye on their small children. They would walk with them to school and, at the end of the day, they met them at the gates to walk them back home again; they were also with them when they wanted to play with their friends in the park. But in Kexbrough, everyone knew almost everyone else and so they never thought that there would be any danger for their kids in such a friendly place. Their mistaken belief that all children were safe in our town was severely shaken when a crime hit the newspapers, which had them talking about the case for a very long time.

None of the names of the witnesses, who were all

underage, were printed in the newspapers, nor did anyone know who had been harmed as it was a closed court. The man who almost everyone in our town had trusted had no choice but to plead guilty to charges of grooming and the sexual abuse of children. Even now, I have images of what happened flickering like a film inside my head.

It was during my summer holidays, aged 11, that my innocence was stolen from me. There were questions I was asked. Ones that I refused to answer, just as children who are victims often don't. Instead, it was the night terrors that crawled into my sleep, making me cry out for help. But those came later. Even all these years later, those dark memories of what happened to me that summer still jump into my head. However much I try to blank out all my past trauma, those images still won't leave me alone.

9

It was just as the long summer holiday was due to start that one of our neighbours, John, came to see Mum. He was a dark-haired, tall and good-looking man, aged about 30, who always seemed friendly as well as very smart. Mum seemed impressed by his visit and asked if he would like a cup of tea. My friend Rob was also visiting and we were just about to go out, but I heard John say yes to tea and, before we could leave, he gave us a wide, friendly smile and asked a couple of questions, which slowed us from making our exit.

'I see you have your friend with you, Marc,' he said and then, turning to Rob, he asked him his name. When Rob told him, he smiled.

'You two look like good friends, so are you?'

'Yes!' we said in unison.

'Got any plans for the holidays, boys?'

'No, not really,' Mum answered awkwardly as money

was tight and before I could say playing outside or going to the park.

'I'm not surprised you're not going away this year – I know many people are worried about all these problems that could jeopardise the future of our mines. I keep hearing talk about it,' he told us.

'Yes, my husband is fairly tied up with that now,' I heard Mum say, although I had no idea then what the reason was.

'Now, boys, seeing as you're not going away, I'm going to tell your mother about an idea I have and then you can tell me if it's something you would be interested in,' John announced.

More smiles were shared with us all.

'Now you've made me curious, John. Let me get the tea and you can explain,' said Mum. She turned to me then and said, 'Marc, take John and Rob into the sitting room and I'll bring in the tea and some orange squash for you two.'

The three of us went into the sitting room and sat down on chairs near the small round table where the cups and glasses were always put. Naturally, Rob and I were eager to hear more, but we guessed there was no point in asking John until Mum came back in the room. It was only a few minutes before she did, carrying a tray with cups of tea, glasses of squash and a plate of biscuits.

While sipping our squash and nibbling on biscuits, we kept quiet so that we could listen to what the adults were saying. The words 'Calthorpe' and 'potato picking' certainly didn't get our interest straight away. That happened when John said the farmers, regardless of the boys' ages, paid the same hourly rate for them all. 'Those farmers are pretty generous with their cash when potatoes need picking. Not only that, delicious meals are provided too as part of the wages.'

Food and money. It was those things that finally got our ears pricking up. I'm sure Mum was quite interested too. John then told us about the evening barbecues the farmers laid on after the potato picking, which sounded even more exciting. The thought of sitting outside with a group of other boys of our age seemed fun to me.

'There are three teenage boys who've been coming for a couple of years. They've learned how to cook outside. They're a cheerful bunch and, between them, they make all the evening meals for the others in the group. They told me they want to be chefs one day and this is good practice until they can get their business going.

'All the boys like sitting around the fire as the meat sizzles. It smells delicious as it's being cooked and they can hardly wait for it all to be done so they can pile it on their plates and start eating!'

Now that made Rob and I grin. Everything John was telling us sounded really good. Both of us started thinking that we'd have a really good time if we went to the farm. Not only that, but we hoped that we would come back with our pockets full of money.

John carried on talking about the beauty of the countryside there. All these things made us believe we were going to have a really great summer holiday. Looking back, I can say that it was natural for boys of our age then to like the idea of being somewhere on our own, with no parents to boss us about. We would be responsible for our own work and it would be up to us what time we went to bed. We would be free, wouldn't we? Those were the thoughts running through our heads; thoughts that I would regret well before the trip was over.

'I've been going there every summer for several years,' John told us. 'I think by now you can understand that it's a mix of a working holiday and a fun time. Picking potatoes earns everyone money and it's not a hard job. All the boys I've seen end up with a brilliant suntan, which makes them look like they've been abroad. There's a river near the end of the farm where you'll just love swimming. All the boys I know do. Are you good swimmers?'

'Yes, we both learned to swim at school,' Rob told him. 'The teachers took us to the pool and Marc and me, we were told that we had become good swimmers, especially when we jumped in from the high plank.'

Mum was smiling and looking pleased. She told John that it sounded like a really good summer activity for us.

'You'll enjoy going around with the rest of the group and it looks like your mum thinks the same,' John told us both. 'So, Rob, you need to ask your mum – I can talk to her if you like. If you decide you want to go, just make sure you pack swimming trunks and sun cream.'

The next thing he told us was about the caravans behind the fields where we would be sleeping.

Mum butted in then, 'Where do they get washed and clean their teeth?'

'There are showers just at the side of the caravans. The toilets are out there as well.'

'Sounds like it's all laid on for them,' she said happily, looking over at us.

John began talking about the potato fields themselves. 'The one thing I'll have to show you two – if you decide to go, that is – is how you need to spot the tiny white flowers that cling to the potatoes. I don't suppose you've ever seen them before?'

Of course we hadn't, so we waited for him to explain.

'It's when they're still on the potatoes. You must wait until they're gone and then you can pick them. So, if you walk into a row of flowers, you leave those potatoes because they won't be any larger than a hen's egg. That's all you need to look out for. Now, that wouldn't be difficult, would it?'

'Sounds easy enough,' Rob agreed. 'So, what's the nearest town like? Are we allowed to walk there's when the work's finished?'

'You are, but there are no interesting shops there, if that's what you're thinking. It's a small village, not a big town. All around are farms. A lot of the land is used for breeding animals and growing crops. If you come, I'll be driving through that so you can take a look.'

'Sounds like these two won't be shopping then,' Mum said, laughing. 'It makes me think they'll bring back enough pocket money to last the whole school term!'

'Yes, I'm sure they will,' said John before turning to us and telling us that there would be other boys there about the same age as us.

'So, what do you think then, Marc?' Mum asked. 'Everything John has told us sounds all right to me.'

Well, picking loads of potatoes didn't sound all that exciting, but swimming in the river, eating barbecued meat and bringing home lots of pocket money really made me want to go. Besides, it was far more exciting than hanging around the village. I nodded my head and told her I would like to go.

'How about you, Rob?' she wanted to know.

'I really want to go with Marc,' he said. 'I'll go home and ask Mum. Can she call you if she has any questions? I'm pretty sure she'll say yes, though.'

'Why don't I come with you?' she offered. 'We can talk mum to mum and I bet you'll forget things like showering and teeth cleaning so I can give her all the details so she feels comfortable.'

I knew from her voice that Mum would prefer it if I was going with a friend. She wouldn't want me to feel lonely as, without Rob being with me, I wouldn't know anyone there when I arrived at the farm. Having my best friend there would make those early days a lot easier.

'Hope your mum says yes,' said John, getting up to leave. 'Then I'll be taking the two of you in a couple of days.'

Mum went with Rob to his house while I waited impatiently for the answer. I was relieved and happy when she came back and told me it was all agreed, he was going with me. She also told me that evening that Steve thought it was a good idea too.

Just two days later, John was to pick us up. That day, Steve had already gone to work but he came into my room before he went to say goodbye. 'You have a good time there, Marc,' he said, which surprised me a little.

Once I was up and dressed, I went downstairs to find that Mum was already making breakfast. Rob was sitting at the table, having already eaten his at home.

About half an hour later, John arrived.

'He's here, boys,' Mum announced as she picked up the small suitcase that she had packed for me the night before and brought it out to the car. She gave me a hug and whispered in my ear, 'I'll miss you, my darling, but I really hope you and Rob have a great time there.' She must have noticed how excited I was when I climbed in. I turned my head round and watched her waving to us until the car turned out of our street.

Although that holiday was a long time ago, there's nothing about it that I've been able to forget. Of course, neither of my parents had any idea of the atrocities already planned for me. Do I remember clearly what the journey was like that morning? The answer is yes, I do. Rob and I took turns sitting in the front of the car. When it was my turn, I listened to John telling us all about the farm and the good fun we were going to have there.

We had a break at a café John knew on the way – he told

us that he always stopped there every time he was going to the farm. Inside, glasses of fizzy drinks came first and then plates of sausages and eggs were placed in front of us. While we tucked in, Rob and I enjoyed the stories that John was telling us about the other boys who had been coming each year: 'You two are going to have such a good time,' he kept saying and we believed him. We could hardly wait to see the farm and the caravans we would be staying in.

Back in the car we went, pressing our noses against the windows as we kept hoping to see the farm come into view. When we reached Cowthorpe, with its charming dark-stone houses set in the rolling Pennine foothills, we were really impressed. John then drove down a winding lane, telling us that all the fields we could see were part of the farm. The first ones we passed – hay – had been harvested into tidy, oblong golden blocks. Other fields we liked the look of had both cows and pretty dark-brown calves grazing in them. Next, we came to some larger potato fields, which were not so interesting to us as the other ones.

'Those are the fields you'll be walking to tomorrow,' John told us.

Studying them, we could see those little white flowers on some of the plants that he had told us about.

In just a few more minutes, John pulled up to where the caravans were. There were canvas chairs outside and some sort of table and a large BBQ grill resting on bricks over a pit for the coals.

'That's where your caravan is, boys,' he said, pointing to

a dark-cream vehicle with a couple of steps outside. 'There's another boy who will be sharing with you but he's out working now. He knows you two are coming, so don't worry about that. The barbecue will be set up here this evening so you'll meet him then. Now, I've got to get going, but I need to have a chat with the farmer first.'

He pulled our suitcases out from the boot of his car and carried them into the caravan for us.

'You can sort out your things and then relax and sit outside in the sun for a while. The others will turn up a bit later, and if I don't see you this evening, then I will in the morning.'

'Thanks, John,' we both said.

We hadn't brought much with us so it was easy to stash our shorts, T-shirts, socks and underwear into the drawers. It was easy to spot which ones were our beds as the other bed was a bit messy and had some magazines beside it.

Afterwards, we did as John suggested and sat down on those chairs and gazed up at the bright-blue sky above us. There wasn't a cloud. I could feel the heat from the sun and wished we knew the way to the river.

'If the weather stays like this, we'll get a good tan, won't we?' Rob said.

'Yeah, our mates will think we've been abroad for weeks!'

That thought made us laugh.

'We've got a river to swim in too. Bet it's better than the pool at home. That's always packed. I can't wait to go there!' said Rob excitedly.

We laughed again, already thinking that the place we were

in was great. Soon, we decided to have a walk around and take a look at the showers. With their sturdy wooden planks to stand on, we liked the look of them. The toilets were the next place we came across and they seemed OK too. We must have been there for about an hour when the first boy, who had ginger hair and a broad Scottish accent, turned up.

'I heard you two were coming,' he said and introduced himself as Leo. 'Which one of you is Marc?'

'That's me,' I said.

'Then you must be Rob,' he said, turning to my friend and smiling.

We chatted for a while. Leo told us that he was 15, which I had already worked out because he must have been at least a couple of years older than us. The age difference didn't stop me from taking an immediate liking to him, though.

'You two are from Yorkshire, aren't you?'

I told him that we were and then asked where he had come from.

'I'm from Scotland, up near Glasgow,' he said. 'Some people think it's a bit rough up there, but I don't see it – I have loads of friends there.'

'Do you come here just because you want to earn some money or is it because you like this part of England?' Rob asked.

'A bit of both,' he said. 'I get on well with the others who come, but I do miss my friends back home. My dad persuaded me to come – he thinks it's good for me to spend my holidays working here.'

There was something in the tone of Leo's voice that made me think he wished he didn't have to be there.

'Well, we heard everyone is happy here. At least that's what John told us anyhow,' I said.

I noticed an uneasy expression on his face.

'It's all right around here,' he insisted. 'Just be careful not to wander off on your own. It's always better if we stay with the group.'

'Why's that?' I wanted to know.

'You might get lost, I suppose,' came the answer. 'If I were you, I would stick together and stay with all the younger boys working here. I'm one of them too, which is why we're sharing the caravan together. As soon as we've had breakfast, you can walk to the fields with me every morning if you like.'

In his own way, Leo was giving us a serious message. It only took a few days for him to realise that I hadn't taken any notice of this warning. I'm sure what happened next must have upset him a lot. From what I know, he felt guilty that he hadn't given us a better understanding of why we shouldn't go out without the other boys around us – I suppose he didn't dare say any more. I was only just 11 and too naive to realise what he was trying to tell us.

It was not long afterwards that three boys who were well into their teens turned up. Talk about noise! Still, they were all friendly and we all introduced ourselves.

'We're the ones who have to get the barbecue going, so watch and learn, boys!' Patrick told us.

We soon saw that they were good at getting it alight and

then more boys arrived, bringing large plastic containers with our evening meal marinating inside. When the flames died down and the coals had started to turn from red to white-hot, they told us that the barbecue was ready for cooking. The lids on the containers were removed and tons of meat and chicken, as well as sausages, were placed on the grill.

'We learned how to cook on the barbecue last year,' one of the boys told us proudly.

Now bottles of beer and cans of non-alcoholic drinks were being passed around.

Rob and I really enjoyed our first meal there – the atmosphere was alive with lots of talk about the work on the farm, as well as plenty of jokes from the older boys. Some of them were quite crude and a few just puzzled us but, eager to fit in, we joined in with the laughter all the same.

At the end of the evening, the three of us went into our caravan. Rob and I climbed into our beds after remembering our mums' instructions to clean our teeth, while Leo set an alarm clock.

'We'll need that,' he said. 'Stops us sleeping in too late.'

We slept well and had just about managed to get up when one of the boys banged on our caravan and shouted out that breakfast would be brought over in 20 minutes. That got us all rushing to the showers. They were powerful enough to quickly get us wide awake. Shorts and T-shirts were pulled on just before a cooked breakfast arrived. All the food was nice and hot and, as the weather was still sunny, we were happy sitting outside to eat it.

After that was finished, we made our beds and tidied up, then trotted along to the fields with the older boys. They showed us how to look for the potato plants where the tiny flowers had gone, explaining that those were the ones now ready to be picked. After that, they took us to a row of potatoes that was clear of blossom. Rob and I squatted down and started picking. We could see that the older boys were a lot faster than us, but then they had experience. It took nearly a week before our load was equal to theirs. That pleased not only us, but the other boys as well.

'Good on you two. You've got it nailed!' one of them told us cheerfully.

The evenings were warm, the food at breakfast and from the barbecues tasty. The teenagers had music that they could blast out because there was no one to tell them to keep the noise down or remind them about the neighbours. Bottles of beer were passed around but Leo, Rob and I were only given a very small amount before they handed us lemonade.

'Can't have you youngsters drunk!' Patrick said, which made most of the boys laugh loudly, and by the end of the evening, they were none too sober.

When Sunday arrived, and with the bright rays of sun above our heads, we didn't have work to do, so we all decided to go down to the river.

'You don't want to miss out on swimming there during your stay,' Patrick said to us. 'Can't bank on the weather being sunny every day, can we?'

'I guess not,' Rob answered, shooting me a look which meant 'let's go'.

That was enough for the three of us to go racing back to our caravan, where we put on our swimming trunks under our shorts.

The river looked wonderful when we got there. Off went our shorts and in we jumped. Most of us were good swimmers, though, as the water was not deep, we were all quite safe there. A couple of the older boys were swimming near us and we heard one of them say, 'See who's watching us.' Heads turned. I also looked back and saw it was John.

'Oh, he likes seeing little boys without much on,' I heard one of the older lads say.

Leo, who was swimming between Rob and I, joined in the laughter a little – not that he said anything to us.

That was such a good day. I enjoyed every minute. Sadly, it was the last day of my feeling safe there.

10

The following morning, it was John and not one of the boys who came banging on our door to make sure we were all awake. When Leo saw it was him, I could see instant hate on his face. I also thought he looked a bit frightened, not that I knew why then.

John left soon afterwards. As usual, we went to shower, got dressed and had our breakfast together outside. Once breakfast was over, Rob and I were ready to make our way to the fields when John suddenly appeared and caught hold of my arm.

'Morning, Marc. I see you've got a good tan already.'

'Yes, I like the fresh air out here.'

He smiled at Rob and me and told us he could tell we liked swimming. Out of the corner of my eye, I could see Leo was unhappy at us talking to John. Not that I understood why until just a few hours later. I noticed that John ignored him and only talked to us two. Leo gave us one more look, then began walking with the rest of the group towards the fields.

'Rob, you go with them,' John said. 'I've got a little job for Marc over here.'

My friend looked a bit curious but he didn't ask what the job was before he, too, set off quickly so that he could catch up with the others.

'Stay here, Marc, until these breakfast dishes are cleared up and ready to be taken away, then I'm free,' John told me. 'I thought you could come walking with me to another part of the farm. You'll still get paid for the time because I'll need some help.'

'All right then,' I said and sat back down again.

If only I had been a little older, I might have asked him what I had to do, but I didn't. Of course, at that age I had no reason to be suspicious as to why he wanted to separate me from the other boys and just take me with him. If only I had understood Leo's warning, I might have refused, but I didn't. Unfortunately for me, I would soon find out what he had in mind.

'Which part of the farm are we going to?' I asked when John had finished putting the dishes back in their metal box. I was hoping it might be near the field where some of the cows were grazing with their calves.

'You'll see for yourself very soon,' he told me. 'We'll walk through the woods to get to it.'

The woods were thick with trees while on the grass between their canopy were dozens of yellow buttercups – I thought they were beautiful. As we walked together, John held my arm and he chatted away, pointing out the birds that flew above. After we had walked a while, he started to question me about my parents. It was Steve he most wanted to know about – his questions seemed to focus on how well I got on with him.

I now think he must have heard gossip about the rows between Mum and Steve and maybe he knew that he was not my real father. He let me know that he already had some insight into my home life.

'I heard you have a few problems with Steve,' he said, giving my hand a light squeeze.

He seemed so nice then – the first nice man I'd met in a long time – and I blurted out far too much. I told him that Steve loved his children but that he didn't really want me there. If that wasn't bad enough, I also told him that he could be quite violent and often frightened both Mum and me. In my innocence, I had no idea what was happening.

'Do you have any secrets that he doesn't know about, Marc?'

'No, I don't think so.'

'But if you had, would you let him know?'

'Of course not. Anyhow, I try and keep out of his way as much as possible.'

'Well, you know I live near you so you can always come and visit me,' he said as he put his arm around my shoulders and gave me a hug.

Over the next few minutes as we continued walking, I felt that he cared for me, which gave me a sense of contentment. But it only took a few minutes more for that feeling to change to one of fear.

'I need to pee,' he told me as he let his arm drop from my shoulders and walked over to one of the trees.

I watched as he walked and then felt embarrassed as I realised why his hand was lowering down to his flies. That made me quickly turn my back on him. I made myself look up through the branches of trees to the blue sky, but when I heard him calling me, without thinking what the reason could be, I began walking over. His head was turned towards me and he gave me a friendly smile. Smile or not, I shuddered when I noticed that his flies had not been zipped up. I nearly shut my eyes so that I could stop seeing far too much of those adult parts of his. They were ugly, I thought, and they looked different to mine. I'm sure my face must have been bright red by then. I almost told him about his zip, but thinking he might be embarrassed about forgetting it, I didn't. Now, of course, I know this was all done on purpose.

'Come closer, Marc,' he told me.

I just about gulped – I hadn't the nerve to refuse or give him a hint of what I could see.

'I think that I must have been bitten by some insect and I need you to take a look for me.'

Now his finger was pointing to that part of him, a part I didn't want to see or be anywhere near. I didn't know what to do so I just stared at him, wordless. Before I could tell him that I didn't want to touch him there, he seized my hand and drew it into his trousers. Within seconds, he made my little fingers clasp hold of that part of him, pressing them until they were forced to curl around his large, hard penis. Then he moved my hand up and down briskly until, after a short time, I could hear him gasping. Of course, then I didn't know what that meant. At least he had let my fingers go, but that didn't stop me from feeling sick. I thought then that it was all over, but I was wrong there. What he did to me next was even worse.

'Now, let's do the same for you, Marc,' he said.

Leaning down slightly, his large hand caught hold of the zip on my shorts and pulled it down. I wanted to try to get away from him, but his other hand was now holding onto my shoulder to make sure I couldn't move.

I don't think I need to describe here what happened next. At that age, I was both appalled and terrified – I just wanted to wriggle away from him and run for my life. But where could I have run to? I was so shaky after he stopped squeezing that small part of my body that I tripped over the roots of that tree. Grass stains and dirt were all over my shorts and my knees were grazed as well. John pulled me up and told me we would walk back slowly – 'Can't have you falling again.' My stomach was churning and my legs remained wobbly as we made our way out of the woods.

Of course, John would not want to take a boy back to the camp who appeared upset and frightened. So, what did he do? He talked about money.

'I told you that you'd make more money with me than working in the fields, didn't I?' he began.

I heard him, but I was unable to answer.

'Look, Marc, I always stick to my word so here you are now, put this in your pocket,' and he handed me a couple of notes. As his fingers briefly touched mine, I visibly flinched, though I still said nothing.

I suppose had I been older, I might have sworn and tossed the notes back at him, but not knowing quite what to do, I just stuffed them in my pocket.

It was when I could tell that we were near our caravan that John gave me another smile. 'Almost there, lad,' he said. 'I've got to go to my office, so you can run off to your caravan if you like. No need to go to the fields.'

Shamefaced, I could scarcely look up at him. It came as a slight relief that I could go back to the caravan on my own. He let go of my arm and, without saying anything, I turned and ran as fast as I could to the safety of the caravan. *Thank goodness there's no one else here,* I thought. All I wanted was to shower and feel clean again. I ran in, grabbed a bar of soap and a large towel and then took myself off to one of the cubicles. After turning on the water as fast and as hot as I could, I got underneath and scrubbed frantically at my body until my skin stung. I even rinsed my shorts and T-shirt out under the water – luckily, I had some more clothes in the caravan. I wrapped myself in the towel then went back to the caravan and pulled on clean clothes before I put my wet clothes on the washing line to dry.

It wasn't much longer after I had got back when our group arrived with lunch. Naturally, they asked where I had been with John. I told them that we had to go to the farm and collect a few things. That was all. I couldn't bring myself to tell anyone what had happened, not even Rob. I was just so ashamed and equally confused. At the age I was then, I couldn't understand why a man who my mother had grown to like and trusted had touched me like he had. While those thoughts were running around my head, I noticed Leo gazing intently towards me. He must have noticed that I had changed clothes and, in retrospect, I think he would have guessed what was happening to me.

A little later when it was just Leo and me in the caravan, he asked me if I was all right. I managed to make my mouth go into a smile and said yes but I didn't elaborate. I don't think for one moment that he believed me.

So, did the abuse happen just once? No, I'm ashamed to admit that I stayed at the farm for another four weeks and John took me with him into the woods at least once a week. Why did I not tell someone what was happening? Of course, I know now that he would have been fired immediately and I would have been looked after but, at the time, I was too frightened. Even now I can't bring myself to describe everything he did. Let's just say when we finally left the farm, my mind was hurting me, even more than the soreness in the parts of my body which he had assaulted.

If people knew then, I'm sure they would have asked why, after that first time you were molested, didn't you just ring your parents and ask them to come and get you? They might not have understood that I simply couldn't bring myself to speak about it. With hindsight, I now know that just one call to Mum and Steve would have got them there immediately.

The answer to why I didn't do that is known both by the police and child therapists. Children never want to talk about those adult crimes – the humiliation engulfs them so deeply, they blame themselves more than they blame their molester. It can take some time for a skilful and highly trained but gentle therapist to encourage abused kids to talk. They understand when others don't always know that it takes time for a child to be able to reveal the truth, though in my case, it was a little different as it was not a therapist who managed to find out what had happened to me.

I can remember our drive back home on that high summer day very clearly. I couldn't even take pleasure in the money I had saved from all the notes that John had thrust in my hand. Rob talked away about how he was going to spend his savings so I did my best to sound as though I, too, was pleased. He had said how much he had in his pocket and I simply uttered that it was about the same as me. It was an obvious lie as John had handed me extra notes every week, ones that I would have to hide. He had also told me on the last occasion that any time I visited him at his home, there would be more money in it for me.

Nothing, not money, not anything, would tempt me to go to his house – I never wanted to see him again. When I arrived home and he handed me my suitcase from the boot of his car, I could tell his eyes were appraising me again.

Not that he could do anything more then as Rob was still in the car. I think he deliberately let me out first so that I would hopefully appear happy when I got into the house.

Hearing the car pull up, Mum came to the door and hugged me while telling me my suntan looked good.

'Must have been great, darling.'

'Yes, Mum,' was the only answer that I could bring myself to say.

The evening with Mum and Steve was pleasant enough. Or should I say it might have been if I didn't have so much to cover up. I tried not to cringe when so many questions came my way and managed to keep telling my parents how much fun the evenings were. My little brother and sister were curious as well, I could tell. So, I told them about swimming in the river.

It was when I was upstairs on my own that I kept imagining Leo. *Think of what he said to you – he knew about John and was trying his best to stop you going with him to the woods that day.* My inner voice kept telling me this over and over. For hadn't Leo tried to say, 'I don't want you to leave our group behind?' So, what did he know? Had he gone through the same things as me?

I kept seeing the expression on Leo's face when John took me out that first time.

'I don't like him,' was all he said when I asked, but somehow, I felt that he knew all too well about John's passion for underage boys. The older boys had already said that he liked watching boys with only swimming trunks on, or better still, when they pulled them off when they emerged from the water and put dry shorts on.

I really wished Mum wouldn't keep saying such nice things about John and how pleased she was that he had taken Rob and me to the farm. All I could hope was that he wouldn't come to our house to see us again, or worse, that they actually invited him round. Just the thought of having to be polite to him made me feel anxious and stressed.

From what I can remember now, it was about a week after I had arrived home when I saw a police car pulling up outside our house. Steve must have seen the car as well as he moved quickly to the door. I heard a woman's voice saying that she wanted to have a chat with my parents and my face went bright red as soon as I heard the word 'farm'.

Steve must have stepped outside then as I couldn't catch any more of their conversation – I suppose he didn't want Mum and me to hear what it was about. But then Mum came into the living room and looked startled when she saw that Steve was outside on the pavement talking earnestly with the policewoman and a young constable.

It must have been only a couple of minutes later when Steve came back inside and told me to go upstairs because he and Mum had to talk to the police in private. I didn't know then that they were requesting their permission to question me about my time at the farm. Apparently, Steve didn't want that to happen then and there as he wanted to know a little more from me first. Or rather he wanted to know if I had been that man's victim before I answered any questions from the police.

Why are they here and what do they want? My head was full of questions. I kept my bedroom door open because I wanted my sharp ears to try to hear what they were talking about, but I could only pick out a few words. It was when I heard the policewoman say John's name that I felt really frightened. If it was something about him, then I knew why they were there. Was I in trouble? It was Steve who, after a few minutes, came up to my room. Having heard his footsteps on the stairs, I jumped into bed and covered myself with my duvet – I wanted him to think that I had fallen asleep, but that didn't work.

'You can't disappear, Marc,' he said, for once quite gently. 'I want you to come down. They have a few questions for you.'

I panicked then.

Seeing the expression on my face, Steve took hold of my hand.

'Look, don't get worried now. They don't think you've done anything wrong and they're not going to ask you anything difficult. They just want to know about your time with John.'

'What about him?' I wanted to ask him, but I couldn't get any words out.

'They've heard he used to take you for walks in the forest. Why was that, lad?'

That made me want to shrink against the mattress and so I pulled the duvet over my head.

Undeterred, Steve sat down on the bed and rested his hand on my shoulder before he asked me if John had ever touched me. There was a sadness and an irony that it took something as awful as what happened to me for my stepfather to show an ounce of care towards me. It just made me feel worse.

'Look, you can tell me first if he did anything to you – I'm talking about the part of your body between your legs.'

Before I could say that John hadn't touched me, Steve added gently, 'If he did, none of it's your fault – there are some horrible people who want to do things that no one likes. So, all you have to do is say yes, he did, when you were in the woods and I will try and help you feel better, Marc.'

I could feel my face burning again as the image of John with that smile of his when his flies were open entered my head. But still, I said no, he hadn't touched me; that he had just taken me for walks.

'I'll have to tell the police that then,' he told me. 'But one more question: are you really telling me the truth?'

'Yes,' I said and I tried my hardest not to let the tears start forming, betraying my lies. I felt so bad then as I could tell from the look in Steve's eyes that he didn't believe me.

'They've asked other boys the same question and most of them said the same as you, Marc. But there's one boy who has told the police that he would refuse to go back to the farm if John was there. Whichever boy it was, he reported the man to the police. He actually took himself to the station and asked to speak to a duty officer.'

Steve didn't tell me everything then. Evidently, John had told the police that there were other reasons why that boy did not want to work at the farm. He just had a whole group of friends he wanted to spend his summers with and the boy's father was insisting he went back, whether he liked it or not, for most of his next school holiday. That was John's defence – he was being used as an excuse. The boy, however, told the police that he had kept quiet about two of his holidays there, but if he didn't speak up now, even more young boys would be harmed.

I was told later that the police thought getting John to court on the evidence of only one boy would be more difficult. So, why did they come to my house? It was because the boy who had talked had also given details about me being taken into the woods.

'Who is the boy?' I asked, although I guessed it must be Leo. I wished I had his phone number, but I didn't.

'They won't give his name, Marc, because whoever the boy is, he's underage. But he was there at the same time as you. I know he told the police that he was not the only one who had suffered from what the police call "abuse". The police and the parents want to put away a man like that so he'll never be able to touch a child again.'

I felt so dirty for what John had done to me and I also had guilty feelings for not telling Steve the truth. I know now that I was like so many abused children who deny and deny that they've been molested. Like me, they feel it is to their shame that they haven't gone to an adult who can put a stop to it immediately.

Steve was kind enough. He just said, 'Well, stay up here and I'll talk to the police. All right, Marc?'

I wasn't all right, though. Not that I said so.

I think now that Steve must have told the police that he knew I hadn't just gone for a walk with John, but if we all waited a while, he was confident I would finally talk. I'm sure it's done differently these days, but that's the way things worked back then.

While I lay in bed, I thought about Leo and the courage he had had in telling the police about what had happened to him the two summers before. I remembered the expression on his face that day when John ignored him and took hold of my arm. Leo must have gone through what I had and guessed what had happened to me. It must have been hell for him, knowing what was about to take place. I knew he saw that I was distressed and that was why he kept asking me later that day if something was troubling me. I just shook my head, but he knew – he'd already spotted my clothes drying on the line.

I felt so guilty; why couldn't I be as brave as Leo?

11

Mum and Steve said nothing more about why the police had come to our house. There was certainly peace there then. Not one further question about the farm came up. I managed to talk about the good things there, such as the barbecues and the days we went swimming, though even they reminded me of John watching us boys – and particularly me.

It only took a few more days for me to break down. Nightmares that had John in them woke me and hot angry tears ran down my cheeks. I took a deep breath, curled up tight and tried to fall asleep again. Maybe it was also my guilt for not backing Leo? Somehow I managed to go back to sleep and that was when the night terrors returned. I must have screamed out loud because something woke Steve and Mum up. She came into my room and, seeing the tears that were running down my face, she put her arms around my shoulders and pulled me to her. I heard her telling me gently, 'You're all right, Marc. I'm here.'

My eyes opened and then I saw that Steve was standing behind her. He amazed me by sitting on the end of my bed and asking me what my nightmare had been about.

That's when I burst into tears again.

'It was about the farm, wasn't it, Marc? You can tell us now, can't you?' He bent slightly towards me and took hold of my hand and wrapped his fingers around it, squeezing it gently.

'You need to get the poison out of your mind. That's something I do know is necessary to stop nightmares. You tell us the truth of what happened in Cowthorpe and it will be the last time you find yourself screaming in your sleep and you can then begin to feel much better.'

So, I took a deep breath and managed to tell them about how John began taking hold of me on that first walk.

'But he did it more than once, didn't he?' said Steve.

I could tell by his expression that he knew it had happened quite a few times. I gulped as I admitted that John had made me go out for a walk with him every week into the woods and the same things happened each time.

'He kept giving me money as though I wanted to go with him so that I could earn it. It made me feel that I was dirty each time he tucked notes into my hands. I didn't want them. That's why I've hidden the money in the cupboard.'

'You mean it's not together with your savings?'

'No.'

Mum was beginning to look a bit tearful by then.

'That man needs to go to prison,' said Steve firmly.

'I'm going to let the police know the harm he's done to you. Maybe they can get his fingerprints off the cash.'

I hadn't realised that molesting children got people into prison. Steve explained what a crime it was and how those adults force children not to talk about what they've done to them.

'Do you understand now?' he said.

'Yes, but when I was at the farm, I thought they could do what they wanted.'

'John is an adult man. You are still a child. If he's messed around with underage kids, it's a serious crime. No one's going to harm you like that again, I'll make sure of it. So, if any man tries anything again, just let them know you would tell me. OK, Marc, have you got that?'

'Yes,' I said.

'I'll tell the police that they can talk to you when you're feeling a bit better then.' He squeezed my hand gently again. 'Now your mum and I will stay here until you go back to sleep. It's almost dawn but you can have a lie-in.'

Mum tucked me in then, kissed the top of my head and wrapped the bedding tightly around me.

What I didn't know until later was that Steve had a reason for telling the police that I wasn't very well but that hopefully I would be all right to talk to them in 24 hours. Then if I was better, he would bring me in.

It was Mum who explained what Steve and the inspector had said to each other. My parents told him that, of course, they would want to have me seen by a child therapist, a professional who was used to getting answers from abused children. The inspector also understood that boys, often more than girls, are usually too embarrassed to tell their parents everything that has gone on so that's why the police must be very careful about how they frame questions.

The morning I was due to go to the police station, Mum told me that Steve had to go out, but he would be back soon.

'He'll be there to look after you at the station, so you have nothing to worry about.'

It was a while before I found out what Steve had been up to. His plan was that, before the police came knocking on John's door again, he wanted to tackle him and scare the life out of him. He wasn't going to go round to John's house and tell him off on his doorstep. Instead, he waited in his car until he saw him walking over the motorway bridge and drove the car straight at him.

Seeing that car coming at speed, with Steve's furious face leaning forward over the steering wheel, must have made John think that he was about to be killed. Of course, he would have known the reason why. Steve braked at the last moment and then got out of the car and grabbed hold of John. We don't know who saw that incident, but the gossip went round our village like wildfire. What Steve said to him no one knew but you can probably guess what it was. Confess or the fathers of the village would have him beaten up. There would be more damages than a few bruises. The fury on Steve's face would have told him that there was nothing he could say to wriggle out of it.

* * *

When Steve came back in, he appeared calm and friendly.

'Right, Marc, time for me to take you to the police station. I can tell you now that everything will be all right. No chance of John approaching you in the future.'

I followed him out, got in the car and we drove to the station.

The inspector introduced me to a woman who was the one I needed to talk to. I found being with her was a lot easier than having to talk to a man in a uniform that I didn't know. The woman was about Mum's age, with thick blonde hair and a pleasant smile, which made me a little more relaxed. She was not in uniform and was dressed casually in cream trousers and a blue jumper.

The room we were in had a few comfy chairs and a small coffee table like Mum's. Once we were sitting down, the woman brought up a few questions but in a way that was tactful enough for me not to squirm with embarrassment. She explained that she was a therapist and she worked with young people who had some problems, then she got me a fruit juice to drink while we were together in that room. After that, she made notes and managed to get me chatting to her about the farm, both the good times and the bad ones. When she had finished, she took me out to Steve and said how well I had done. I could hardly believe an hour had passed by.

John was arrested that day. Steve told me that it was my

statement that had clinched the case. From what I heard later, it was his confession that put him in prison.

Steve arranged for me to continue to see the same therapist for a while – he felt I needed some kind of help that he and Mum weren't able to give me themselves. Whatever had occurred, it was a kindness rarely shown and it helped me a great deal but it also created a conflict in my life that would tear me even more apart than before.

12

For some time after John was found guilty, Steve continued to be very kind to me. Life at home seemed peaceful for a while. Since he had known how John had treated me, my stepfather had been extremely thoughtful as well as protective of me. If he hadn't tackled John like he did, maybe John wouldn't have confessed and then I would have had to go to court and tell the judge the details of him molesting me. That was hardly something I would have found easy; I doubt any child would. In fact, I would have been really frightened while I waited for the court date and as I sat outside waiting to go into the courtroom.

I had to admire what Steve had done, making John admit his guilt so that I didn't have to be questioned again. I was pretty certain that the whole of Kexbrough knew how he had got John to confess. Almost everyone seemed to respect and admire him for what he had done.

It was the way he managed to get me to open up and talk

about what happened that made me feel he had grown much fonder of me. Somehow, though, I had my doubts about Steve's good temper and his kindness lasting for long. I don't know why, but I had the feeling that our world was going to change again. There were several things that made the back of my neck prickle. Mainly, it was when I remembered Steve talking about the miners' strikes and the terrible effects they had had on people ten years ago. It seemed to me that, underneath his smile, he was worried that it was all happening again. He had told us about the sadness of the people and how their lives were ruined. Then there were the number of meetings he had. There must be a reason for them. I could only hope that the government was not going to close the pits down and ruin all our friends' lives. I suppose, at the age I was then, I shouldn't have heard so much about men losing their jobs. I made myself push the details of what had happened before to the back of my head – I knew it would be wrong to talk about such things at school.

At least Steve wasn't talking about strikes now. He seemed more relaxed. I had begun to like the way he chatted more to me than he had done before that holiday. He even asked if I would like to go out with him and Mum to the miners' club at the weekend.

I must have gasped with delight at being asked to spend an evening with them there. 'Oh yes, please,' I said, which made both of them smile.

Once we had all had an early tea on the Saturday, I rushed to my room so that I could put on my smartest trousers as well as a clean shirt. After I had changed into my only decent outfit, the next task was to get my hair smooth. Looking at myself in the mirror, I brushed and brushed my hair until, finally, it looked really neat. That made me feel I was ready then to join Steve and Mum downstairs. As I went into the sitting room, I heard both of them say how smart I looked. I felt my face burn a little when I heard that.

It was not long after I had come down when Hazel, the daughter of one of my mother's friends, turned up. She was there to keep an eye on my little brother and sister until we all got back. Much as I loved them, I was happy to be going out with Mum and Steve instead of staying in and keeping an eye on them. Usually, it was me who had to stay in with them – not that I didn't have some fun with them both.

It was when we had entered the club and were walking over to a table that I heard the name 'John' a few times. He must have been the talk of the place. At least no one said anything about him in front of us, which saved me from embarrassment. Mum had already told me that he had been sent to prison and, as his house was rented out, he wouldn't be back for some time. I suppose that, as everyone in Kexbrough knew, he would have to move away – the gossip would not make him welcome back in our community.

As the whole town had heard what Steve had done to get John to admit his crimes, they must have thought there must be a reason for the attack. Looking back, I'm sure a lot of people would have worked out that I must have been one of the kids who had been abused. They must have made sure that they were careful when I was near them not to mention the name 'John'.

I dreaded hearing anyone talk about what John had done; I didn't want people who knew I had been taken to the farm by him asking me questions. I suppose that's what I had expected, but thankfully, it didn't take long for me to realise they wouldn't.

But the boys at school couldn't care less about my privacy. After the court case and all the stories about it, which no doubt had become completely exaggerated, there were groups of boys who couldn't stop talking about John and his victims.

When Rob and I went outside in the playground, we heard the other boys talking about 'the monster', which was the nickname they had given to John. What those groups of boys wanted to know was who were John's victims. The details of what they believed he had done to them kept coming out of their mouths. They might have snorted with laughter while I shivered, for they had described just about everything which had happened to me. I felt relieved when a teacher overheard them sniggering about men wanting sex with children. She was furious and the boys were told to stop immediately with their gossip and speculation, otherwise they would be in detention when school finished. Even so, when there were no teachers about, I kept hearing more whisperings about John and the farm. What made it worse was that some of the boys in my class knew Rob and I had gone to the farm where John stayed for some of the summer holidays. Thankfully, it was Rob they asked about how much we knew about him.

I was just walking out of school when Rob signalled me over. Before any of the boys could ask me anything, Rob just said, 'They want to know about John.' With a calm expression on his face, he told them that John had given us both a lift to the farm and brought us back when we had finished there – 'Apart from that, we didn't see much of him. That's right, isn't it, Marc?' And he turned towards me.

'Yes, it is,' I managed to say, although I kept thinking that I might blush.

A knowing look went between us, not that the other boys would have realised it. I knew that Rob was totally aware about my walks with that man, but he had no intention of saying more than what he had already told them. I was so grateful to him in that moment and for being such a good friend too. He must have known what had happened to me back then, but we were still kids and neither of us said a word to the other.

And it was only many years later when we finally did manage to talk about it.

13

There were other nights when Steve and Mum took me with them to the miners' club. I can remember so clearly that we never stayed late, except for the one evening that often makes me smile when it springs to mind. Once inside, the three of us made our way to the bar. Steve ordered a soft drink for me and a couple of beers for Mum and himself. It was on their third drink when Mum nodded over towards the door as she had seen a band coming in. She must have known who the band were, for her smile said it all as she told me excitedly, 'I can't wait to hear them! You'll really enjoy their music, Marc.'

As soon as the band came onto the small stage and began playing, Mum's feet started tapping away. I had a shrewd idea that she didn't want to leave early that night. Still, it was a Saturday, so I could sleep in the next day.

Now, let me mention something cheerful for once. I doubt anyone reading this knows the song 'Woolly Bully' sung by Sam the Sham & The Pharaohs. Not that they were the original group who played the sixties music and sang in the miners' club. It was certainly a good type of 'twisting away' music. I didn't know then that the music and the way people danced to it had come out over 20 years earlier. That band must have really enjoyed copying it and the dance floor soon filled up with people.

It was when the first beat of that song started that Mum, with her tapping feet, slammed down her glass of beer and nodded at Steve. He put down his drink and both of them got up.

'You can watch us jive,' Mum said as she headed off to dance.

They were quickly on the dance floor, jiving away.

I adored my mum and even forgave her when she went back to Steve but I never knew how well she could dance until that night. I was amazed at how both of them moved in unison to the music. Talk about legs kicking out and then a huge swirl of Mum and her fingers managed to tap on the floor! Lots of clapping and a few loud piercing whistles from the crowd; some of the dancing couples even stopped to watch them.

I felt so happy when I heard people saying that Mum's dancing was brilliant and I glowed with pride. I had to smile at Steve's movements, which surprised me – he was pretty good as well. That night was the best I'd ever had with them. At the end of the number, Mum was surrounded by people. They came over and congratulations and hugs were exchanged and were given, as was praise for the way they had danced together. They also chatted to Steve and told him they never thought for a moment that he could dance like that. The compliment made him laugh as well, as he ordered another round of drinks. That rumour about how he had frightened John enough to go to the police and admit his guilt had made my stepfather a lot more popular in our small community.

I had rarely seen Steve so cheerful as on that evening in the club. As for Mum, she was laughing and smiling as she chatted away to everyone near her. This was the mother I seldom saw and, back then, I wanted her to stay like that forever.

Sadly, the mum I saw all too often was the one who was increasingly falling to pieces.

14

Maybe, after all this time, I was hoping that, finally, Steve would see me as his own son. After all, hadn't he been kind to me? But my inner voice told me that him being kind when I had those nightmares didn't mean he saw me the way I so desperately wanted.

Come on, have a look at him when your little brother and sister are there, then you'll see how proud of them he is. There you are with your hopes, but does he treat you the same way as he does his own kids? Why don't you take a look in their bedrooms, then you'll see the difference between their rooms and yours? That should make you jealous!

But it didn't – I simply loved my young brother and sister. I had been given some hope when I had told Steve about what happened to me on the farm and had seen how protective of me he had been. That was the reason I had been feeling that he must be fonder of me than he had been before John's crime.

Now, what about the presents he has given his children? You saw what they were, didn't you, Marc? He put a fancy Hi-Fi in each of their rooms as well as a TV but there's nothing in your room, is there?

I had seen Steve taking everything up to their rooms more than once and had felt so hurt that there was never anything for me. He hadn't even put a small table and chair in my room to make doing my homework easier. There was no point in me going into my siblings' rooms to watch TV with them – they only wanted to see shows for small kids. I tried my best not to feel jealous because I loved them both. The other thing I began to notice was that Steve never seemed to tell them off or complain about the mess they made. Whatever they had done, he just laughed and hugged them. It was those moments when he showed what a good father he was to them that hurt deeply, and even more than I realised.

15

What did I say earlier in my story? I had an uneasy feeling that Steve's bad temper would re-emerge eventually. I was right there, though I could tell that what was happening in mines all over the UK had caused him to be badly stressed. It also affected a lot of other people in Kexbrough. Even around school, I kept hearing the dismal talk of the senior boys, who seemed unsettled by what was taking place. Being the sons of miners, it was understandable that they were worried, not only about themselves, but their families too. The bright ones were studying hard because they were determined to get good results in their exams, which meant they could go on to university and not even consider a job down the mines.

Back then, students were given decent grants and there were no tuition fees so those who came from poorer families could afford to go to university. The other good thing compared to now was that they didn't have to run up a large student debt that must be paid back monthly from their salary once they had started in their careers at a certain level. Even so, with a father out of work, family life would be difficult. Many of those seniors felt there was nothing much they could do to help unless they left school and got a job – any job – rather than pursue their academic ambitions. Fortunately, from what I heard, their parents had told them that they wanted them to be the first in their family to get the college education they deserved – 'We will manage,' they assured them.

At the first signs of my stepfather's temper, I didn't realise straight away what was causing it. I knew a lot of mines across the UK were already closed, but everyone had hoped that the Barnsley pit would be left open. But Steve already knew that all the strikes hadn't worked and so many miners he knew personally, including himself as the union rep, were going to lose their jobs.

The miners who had been working ten years before at the time of the previous strikes were furious with the government for letting it happen again. At least that's what Mum was saying anyway, as she tried to explain to me what was going on. Of course, Steve would have been listening to the radio from the moment he woke up and then reading every newspaper he could when he arrived at the union offices. They were full of articles about the strikes and the reasons why the miners and their wives were so resentful. Closures would mean that hundreds, if not thousands, of men would be losing their jobs. Families would be torn apart.

Mum said that Steve had known for a while that this was going to happen: 'That was what his meetings were all about,

Marc.' As I had never worked in a mine, you might well ask why I'm mentioning the miners' strikes so much in my story – after all, they happened a long time ago when I was still in my early teens. But I've never forgotten the effect they had on so many of the boys at my school, and it had such an effect on Steve's temper and behaviour too. That's why I can remember very clearly how so many men were forced to leave their homes and families and travel to other towns all over the UK to try to find alternative work. Without their fathers being around, many of the boys got in a great deal of trouble; trouble that actually resulted in one boy's death. The older and more ambitious ones managed to get into college. The careers teachers at school were great at suggesting courses for the new era of jobs, such as IT and telecoms. But I began to go around with some of the teenagers who had little idea of what they could possibly aspire to when they left school. Instead of thinking about studying more so they might be able to find decent work, quite a few of them wrecked their futures in a variety of different ways.

I should know all about that – after all, I was one of them.

How all of that happened comes a little later in my narrative. For now, I'm going back to when Steve's rage about Parliament and the UK government quickly seemed to transfer to him raging at Mum and me. None of his temper was directed at his own children, though. As I've said earlier, even when they had done something wrong, they were seldom ticked off. Neither Mum nor I believed that any of Steve's good points would remain, not after the

Barnsley mines started to close. We had heard his phone calls with some of the men who had worked under him and we knew that it wouldn't take long for us to bear the brunt of his rising temper.

Mum always seemed pleased when her friends came over to see us, but I could tell from the expression on his face that Steve resented her popularity and her wide circle. I also suspected that he wanted her to spend more time with his own kids than me. After all, I was not his son. As I grew older, I think that he began to wish I was no longer there. I could tell that he was annoyed when Mum and I would be laughing about something or other – often one of my stories about school.

I knew Mum was always waiting to see if his temper was going to explode again. Of course, she hoped it wouldn't, for there was nothing more he could do about saving the mines. He had tried his best but now Barnsley was scheduled for closure. Perhaps the combination of depression, anxiety and anger can make some men violent towards their family; in his case, it did.

It was a Saturday morning when he finally exploded. It was me he hit first, with hardly any real reason. It started when I got up from the breakfast table to fetch something and Steve yelled at me, 'You're such a spoilt brat! Look how you've left your plate and mug on the table. You expect someone else to clear them up for you, don't you?'

'Sorry, but I was coming back,' I said as I began to walk back to the table. 'I'm going to wash them now.'

'Oh, you will, will you? Aren't you always the one who leaves a mess in this house?'

He jumped up and his spittle struck my cheek as he stepped forward and caught hold of me. My legs almost buckled when his clenched fist slammed into my head. He had never hit me like that before. Shaken, my fear was what might he do to Mum if she annoyed him. He was certainly a different person from the man who had helped me so much after my experiences at the farm. That thump to my head was enough to make me feel dizzy, but I tried not to show it. Instead, I pressed my lips tightly together so that I didn't say anything to aggravate him further.

When he walked away from me, I had a horrible feeling that something far worse was imminent. I knew Mum was upstairs as she always changed all the beds on a Saturday – apart from mine, that is, as I did that myself. She would also tidy upstairs and make sure the bathroom was clean and everyone had fresh towels. Then she would come down carrying all the dirty laundry and start stuffing it in the machine. Once the first load was on, she would sit down to have her first cup of tea and some toast and Marmite.

Out of the corner of my eye, I saw Steve ascend the stairs. *Oh no,* I thought to myself. *He's in a terrible mood and he's going to start a row, even if there's nothing going wrong up there.* I kept hearing nasty arguments between them, which I loathed. Despite this, Mum and Steve kept going out to the pub or the miners' club at weekends, although given the impending closures, they were forced to stay in more. It was mainly because people kept asking Steve about what was going to happen with their jobs but, of course, money was also tight. They knew that nearly everyone in the club was worried about their futures and they had decided it had actually stopped being an enjoyable and relaxing night out. Since they had started staying at home, there were more raised voices. Steve's ever-cantankerous tone dominated. It didn't just annoy me, it was upsetting for my younger siblings as well. This was the prevailing mood in our house and, as soon as Steve went out of the room, I was on high alert.

It only took a couple of minutes before the quarrelling started up and it sounded even worse than all the other times. I moved over to the bottom of the stairs so that I could hear what was happening. My siblings came over to stand by my side. The moment we heard the argument switch to yelling at each other, my brother slipped his little hand in mine. A few seconds later, there were screams from Mum. My brother froze and went so pale that I thought he was about to faint. Meanwhile, my sister seemed petrified. If only I was stronger than Steve; then I would have gone up and hit him. How could I help Mum?

'We should have stayed away all those months ago,' I muttered to myself. I had actually begun to like my stepfather when he was kind to all of us, but that morning, it was the other Steve: the one who was always angry and more than scary. I didn't want to go near him.

Here we go again, I said silently to myself. Then I realised

I was shaking. A realisation was dawning on me: if we didn't get out of there, Mum and I would be living in a constant state of apprehension and fear.

That thought had scarcely formulated when, all of a sudden, we heard a large thump coming through the ceiling. I shuddered and guessed that Mum must have been thrown to the floor. I knew I should go up there to try to protect her, even though Steve would more than likely throw me on the floor as well. Just as I was struggling with my thoughts, I heard his thudding footsteps coming down the stairs. This made me feel even more agitated as I didn't know what he might do when he saw the three of us standing there.

'Bloody bitch!' we heard him mutter as, ignoring us, he walked over to the front door. It must have been the first time ever that he didn't say one word to his kids before he went out. As the door slammed behind him, they looked even more upset. After telling them it would be OK and sending them into the sitting room to play, I went up to see Mum. All I could hope was that she was all right and I shot up the stairs two at a time to check.

I gulped a little when I saw that she was still on the floor. I reached my hand down to hers and, using almost all my strength, I helped her get up and then got her to sit down on the side of the bed.

'Bloody bastard!' I couldn't stop myself from saying this.

Mum looked up at me then and, instead of saying anything about Steve, she began talking.

'You know, Marc, every day I think there's less of me left.

So much of my memory of who I am seems to be fading away.'

At the time, I didn't understand what she meant, but a few months later, I did. No, she didn't have dementia, in case you think that her forgetfulness was telling me that. She had depression and it was one of the early signs of the breakdown she was fighting against.

'We must leave here, Marc,' she said suddenly. 'We'll have to take the other two with us this time. Can't leave them in an empty house. Goodness knows when their father will decide to come back.'

Before I could ask when we were going to leave, she leaned over so that she could pick up the bedroom phone. 'I'm going to talk to Eve now.'

I guessed she was going to ask her friend if we could all go over there to stay. While she was making the call, I left her for a few minutes as I needed to tell my siblings that she was all right and I was going to get her a mug of tea. At least that was my excuse for going back up there again.

'Yes, Marc,' she said with a smile as I took in the sweet tea. 'Eve is happy for us all to go there and we can stay as long as we need. I want to leave this place as soon as possible. You'd best tell your brother and sister that they have to get ready to come with us.'

When I went downstairs again, I only told them we were going to visit Auntie Eve for the rest of the day and we might all stay the night as well – 'So, just pack a few things you need – you know, a toothbrush and a pair of pyjamas and anything else you want to take with you. We'll have a really nice day over there and the sun's shining so you can play in her garden.'

I was hoping that would keep them busy as I didn't want to deal with any more questions. I knew that they wouldn't want to stay there any longer than one night so I didn't mention packing any of their clothes.

The three of us went upstairs and into the bedroom where Mum was. She sat up on the bed and told my siblings everything was all right and that she was going to take them with us to Eve's house – 'A nice visit for the day,' she said with a smile that I saw was taking some effort to summon up. I was relieved that she hadn't told them then that she and I would not be coming back when they returned home.

As they scuttled off to get their things, I asked Mum if she needed help with packing.

'No, you get yourself sorted out and I'll throw my stuff into the big suitcase. Then I'll phone for a taxi to take us all there,' she told me.

This time, surely she won't go back to him, I said to myself. I truly hoped she wouldn't fall into the same trap as before. I knew my siblings were not happy about having to leave their home, even for the day. They couldn't bring their televisions or any of their toys, and even though I had said we were only staying for a night, I don't think my sister believed me. She certainly seemed sceptical when she went downstairs and saw all the stuff that Mum had brought down. Her eyes widened even more when she saw the big suitcase placed next to the front door.

I'm not going into details about us packing here. It was more or less the same as when we stayed at Eve's house before. As I reflected on those three weeks, I remembered how peaceful it had been and how disappointed I was when I found out that she had met up with Steve a couple of times. All I could do was hope that this time of leaving Steve would be the last one, but underneath, I had a feeling that it wouldn't be.

I made up my mind while we were in the taxi that, even if Mum went back to him again, I wouldn't go back under any circumstances. I was certain that one of my aunts or even my Gran would let me stay with them. Much as I loved Mum and my siblings, I just couldn't bear being in a place where there was always trouble. Of course, my brother and sister had no intention of staying away longer than one night. My sister would have understood that Mum couldn't have left them behind as there was no adult in the house.

Eve was very nice to my siblings when we arrived there and both of them seemed all right for most of the day. It was in the evening when they began to ask when they could go home to Daddy, and Mum and I just shrugged. She didn't want any arguments. You could see all the fight had left her body and her mind, so she held out her phone, which my sister grabbed quickly. Mum said she could ring her father as, no doubt, he would arrange to get them back home. My sister made the call – she was the one who loved Steve above all else – and I was not surprised, nor was Mum, when she took the phone out into the hall so that we couldn't hear what she was saying. It didn't take long for her to come back looking happy.

'He's going to send us a taxi,' she told us.

Of course he would. Probably too drunk to drive, I nearly said.

It was me who went out with them and gave them both a hug when the taxi arrived.

During our time at Eve's, I kept waiting for Mum to want to return to the house. Much as I loved my mother, I remembered that the last time she had also told me she would never go back to him, but she had. And that was why I believed she would do the same again.

16

Sometimes it's hard for me to tell my story in strict chronological order. When my memories pop up, I know I need to write them down before the experience of reliving them as if they were yesterday leaves me.

When Mum had a breakdown, it upset all of us so deeply that I find it hard to write about, but it's a fundamental part of my story so I need to do it here in this book. Another such event was when I finally met my father's biological family. I know I need to tell you about that too, but you must be patient with me …

17

After Mum told me that she was going back home, I was more than a little disappointed as I had made up my mind not to go with her. Still, I was not really surprised. I had suspected all along that Steve would have done his best to make her want to be with him again.

This time, we stayed away a couple of weeks longer than before, but that didn't stop me from thinking that she had been meeting up with him more often than she admitted to Eve or me. Oh, of course there had been excuses – ones I didn't believe – and of course she was concerned about her youngest children. Since she came back really late one evening, I didn't think for a moment that she had been out so late with my siblings. Not when I could smell wine on her breath. I badgered her for answers until she admitted that she and Steve had gone out for a meal together.

'Did you enjoy it?' I asked.

Not noticing my irony, she gushed, 'Yes, darling, we

had a really nice evening – he took me to my favourite restaurant too.'

She carried on telling me that it was his kind self that she had been with. I guess that she knew the word 'kind' would make me remember the time Steve had really helped me. And yes, I reluctantly admit here that it did work a little. I remembered that side of his character when I had been with him after he caught John and made him confess to the police. But that was well over two years ago; a time when he could tell jokes that made us all laugh. Also, I suppose he was fairly generous when he had taken Mum and me out to the club.

When Mum told me about Steve being so nice, that still didn't stop me being concerned about her trusting him again. I hadn't forgotten those odd remarks she had come out with after he had thrown her on the floor. Only six weeks ago, she had kept saying things that made me wonder if she really believed her memory was beginning to be a problem. Not that I had noticed her being forgetful at all since she had left Steve.

It didn't take long after that meal out for her to tell me she was going back to her other two children and, of course, him. She hoped that I would go back with her too. I didn't argue with her, apart from saying if she wanted to go back, then it was up to her, but I wouldn't be coming with her. She seemed to accept that and, with a smile, suggested we could meet up some days after school and go out for coffee. Before I could ask if my siblings would mind that, she told me a friend of hers would walk home with them and then stay there until she came back. I could tell she was still hoping that I would change my mind, but I had no intention of doing so.

I remained with Mum's friend Eve for a while as she had assured me that she was happy having me there. Even after Mum's reassurances about Steve's repentance, I still couldn't face living with him again. I was scared for her, but I knew there was nothing I could do to force her to leave him and I couldn't continue to be a witness to it all. It was the pictures in my head of their depressing and repeated arguments that made me refuse to go back with her. Oh, I'm sure he made promises that their life would be good together again. In fact, she did say something like that, but I still had a feeling that it wouldn't take long for the arguments to start all over again. I wanted peace and quiet where I lived, which seldom happened at home when Steve was there. His constant criticism of me had really turned me against him and hitting Mum had been the last straw.

It must have been only a couple of weeks after Mum had gone back home when my little brother came looking for me during break time. He and my sister often came over to the seniors part of the school to have a chat, so I thought nothing of it until I saw that he was really upset. Before I could ask what was wrong, he grabbed hold of my arm. 'Marc, I need to tell you something about Mum.'

'What is it?' I said.

'I think she's very ill,' he told me, tears forming in his eyes.

I gulped, wondering just what had happened.

'Come on, let's go somewhere no one can hear us,' I said

as I put my arm around his shoulders and got us walking away from the noise of the playground. There were some benches near the football pitch and I guided him towards one of them. 'Now that no one's about, you can tell me what's upsetting you at home and why you think Mum's so ill. Has she got a bad cold or something?'

'No, nothing like that. There's something wrong with her. When I saw her this morning, she looked so pale and didn't say a word to us. We had to get our own breakfast. She was just staring at the wall. We think you should come over.'

Hearing that made my stomach turn into knots. I could have asked more questions, but I decided not to. I wondered what had caused this. It was only two days since I had spent some time with her in a café and she seemed happy enough there. She had talked away about how she had enjoyed meeting up with some of her friends again but I noticed that she was careful not to mention Steve. What had happened to make her change so suddenly? I supposed there must have been some sort of argument the night before. Maybe it was her being out with me that might have made Steve angry.

I decided to try to find out if there had been any rows in the house while my siblings were there but my brother just said not since Mum had been back.

'What about Dad?' I persisted. 'Didn't he say something about her not being well this morning? Why didn't he get you breakfast?'

'He went out early, Marc, so maybe he didn't notice that she wasn't looking too good.'

But then I knew my little brother wouldn't dare say anything critical about his father. After these questions, I could see that he was looking even more upset.

'Marc, our sister thinks the same as me, that Mum needs you. Please, won't you come back with us after school finishes?'

When I saw how hopeful he was looking, I was just about to say that I would. Then he began talking really quickly: 'Don't worry about Dad. He won't be in then – he's working in Barnsley. I don't know what he's doing there. I heard him saying to Mum yesterday that there was a lot of paperwork he had to go through in the office.'

I guess he must have thought that I wouldn't go there if Steve was in the house.

'Of course I'll come back with you,' I told him. 'We all love Mum, don't we? Only you must remember I've known her a bit longer than you two.' I smiled and gave him a quick hug. 'Now try and stop worrying about her. Just wait for me at the gates and then the three of us can walk back together.'

'Oh, thank you, Marc. Our sister will be so pleased that you're coming with us,' he said. And for the first time, a small smile came onto his face. He must have been so glad that I was going with them. After that talk, the two of us walked back to our different classrooms and I should think that both of us regret we had not gone straight home. That afternoon, I found it difficult to concentrate in class as I still kept wondering what had happened to Mum.

As soon as the final bell rang, I just about ran to the gates where both my brother and sister were waiting. Much as my sister loved Steve, I could tell she was as anxious about Mum as her brother was. That afternoon, we all walked as fast as we could to get back to her. Once the door was opened, we stepped inside, only to be aware that there were no sounds at all. It was the silence that made me feel tense. Every other time, Mum would have called out when she heard us coming in, and usually, she had the radio on.

My sister put her arm around me so that she could stand up on tiptoes and whisper in my ear. All she was saying was that Mum might still be in the sitting room as she had been asleep in there when she left for school. I had thought maybe she was having a nap upstairs but, after my sister's whisper, I shot into the sitting room.

The moment I saw her lying on the settee with her eyes closed, I began to feel uneasy. I felt even more so when I made myself call out as cheerfully as I could, saying, 'Surprise, Mum! I've come over to see you,' but she still didn't stir. I'll admit that, for just a second, I was afraid that she was dead. *Look at her properly*, my inner voice told me, which made me get closer to her, and then I could tell that she was still breathing. *Thank goodness, Mum, you're still here*, my mind whispered but I still wanted her to wake from that deep sleep of her's.

'Mum, wake up, please,' I kept saying over and over as I gently shook by the shoulders until her eyes began to flutter.

I think it was my voice that made her manage to pull herself up a little, so that she could see if it was me. It was when her eyes caught mine that I saw such a sad, haunted expression in hers and I felt real shock. I was even more concerned a few seconds later when I noticed a few other things about Mum which I had never seen before. By then, her eyes were gliding all over the room. I thought there must be something she wanted in it. Not only that, but it was also just about the first time I had ever seen her hair so messy, her clothes wrinkled and grubby. That was so unlike her as she was always beautifully groomed and washed her hair every morning when she showered. I suspected she hadn't done so for days.

'Is she awake now?' my little brother whispered.

Although her eyes had briefly opened, Mum still hadn't uttered a single word.

'I think she's starting to be,' I said, trying my best to reassure him.

It was when she moved a little, so the light was falling on her, that I noticed the bruises on her arms as well as a large black-and-blue one right under her left eye. Alas, this was not the first time I had seen similar bruises on her. I asked myself then, and I ask myself now, why is it that so many men beat women? It's as though they believe they own their wives and girlfriends and can do whatever they want to them. Yet Steve never hit his daughter, nor his son, because they were the two that he loved so much.

I clenched my fists a little to keep myself calm as I tried again: 'Come on, Mum! Try and keep awake! I'll get you some tea if you can sit up a bit more.' I then bent over a little so that I could put my arms around her and help her wriggle into a sitting position.

I didn't ask why she was so tired as she looked far from well. I was rather annoyed that my siblings hadn't mentioned that there must have been a huge quarrel in the house. Didn't they know that, when I came, I would immediately recognise those bruises as being caused by Steve's fists slamming into her, which I was pretty certain to be the case. Even when I had mentioned getting her some tea, instead of replying, she just gave me a weak smile.

'Mum, I'll pop in the kitchen and make some tea for us,' I said again as I wanted her to say something, but she still didn't.

When I went into the kitchen, my siblings followed me.

'Do you think you can get Mum better?' my sister asked with such an anxious look.

'I don't know yet, but I'm trying – tea might help,' I said, putting three teabags in the pot as quickly as I could. When the tea was ready, I poured it out into two large mugs, placed them on a tray with some biscuits and took the tray into the other room, putting it on her knees. It was then that I noticed that her hand was shaking as she picked her mug up. That really began to trouble me, though I kept my smile going as I didn't want her to see me looking worried.

It was about half an hour later when I became aware that it was not only the bruises from Steve's beating that had made her ill. There was definitely something else going on. To begin with, it was the way she was talking that just didn't make sense. It hit me that I had heard some of it before as she kept repeating the same sentence and then I remembered that, just before we left to go to Eve's, she had said something about losing her memory.

The way she was talking got me thinking there was something really wrong with her mind. Not that I had any idea what was causing it. What I didn't know until my brother told me was that she had fallen asleep well before and he and my sister had left for school that morning, but he didn't know what time she had come downstairs. I began to wonder what sort of illness she might have.

After she had finished her tea, Mum began saying that she wanted to find her wedding photos. For a moment, I thought she meant the ones with Steve – until it was my father's name that she mentioned.

'I've looked everywhere for them,' she kept saying. 'There's one place I didn't think of looking. Maybe they're there.'

It was then that she pointed to the top part of the cupboard; the one I had raided a few years before. I knew there were no photos left up there, but I didn't dare tell her that. Instead, I tried to change the conversation by talking about school because that was all I could think of to get her attention. Instead of getting her off the track, she couldn't stop telling me that she needed those photos. I remember one of her friends telling me that, once she and Steve were getting married, which was a long time ago now, Steve didn't want any of my father's photos in the house he had rented for us. That might not have pleased her, but in a way, I could understand why he wasn't keen to have them all around the house and certainly not on display. But I knew this would not be the right time to try to explain why there weren't any photos in the house. Another idea came into my head: if she wanted those photos, I could ask my grandmother to let us have a few as she was bound to have kept them. Gran was such a helpful person and she loved her daughter dearly so I was pretty sure that she would let me borrow a few to appease Mum.

'Mum, your family are all very kind and I really like Gran a lot. Every time I visit, she always says how pleased she is to see me. I think she will have the same set of photos. I'm certain if I ask, she'll let me bring you some.'

Did that work? Sadly not.

'I can't find them, Marc,' was her reply, which she repeated at least three times as she sat looking directly at that cupboard.

'Didn't you hear what I said, Mum?'

'I don't know what you're talking about,' she told me.

It wasn't that comment that bothered me, it was the confused expression on her face that was beginning to make me feel scared. It was then that I decided she needed help, which was not something I was able to supply. I decided to ring my Auntie Loretta, her oldest sister, who would surely understand more about what was happening to Mum.

I felt that I had to wait until she stopped talking about those photos before I could leave the room and make that call. I certainly didn't want her climbing up on the chair to look for what wasn't there.

To make sure she couldn't get up quickly, I sat down beside her. It was then that I could see she wasn't far from sobbing.

'I think you'd better have another tea, Mum. Just stay here and I'll get you one,' I told her, beckoning for my sister to take my place and nodding a little to reassure her. 'She wants to come and sit by you too, Mum,' I said loudly.

My sister got the message and, with a nice wide smile on her face, she came over and plonked herself down on the other side of Mum, who actually smiled on seeing her daughter looking up at her.

My little brother, guessing from the look I managed to give him, followed me out into the kitchen.

'What do you think, Marc?'

'I just don't want her climbing up on a chair so that she can look in that top cupboard. She's much too shaky and she could have a bad fall if she tried that. I've got to make a call to Auntie Loretta – I want her to come over. I think she'll be better at helping Mum than me.'

'You want me to stop her getting on the chair?'

'Yes, if you think you can.'

'If she starts getting up, I could fall over in front of her. Then she would want me to sit by her. And if I say my knees are hurting, she won't move.'

I smiled at this elaborate idea but nodded my agreement.

'Good idea! Now you go back in there and I'll bring her some more tea. Putting a tray on her lap should keep her sitting there anyhow.'

So, I did as I had done before and placed a tray with biscuits and another large mug of tea on her knees. That would stop her getting up, I thought as I went back to the hall where the phone was. I pulled the sitting-room door almost closed behind me, and once I had dialled the number, I took the handset as far away from the door as possible. It was a good thing that my aunt was in. When I told her about Mum and how I didn't know what to do, she told me to stop worrying.

'Marc, I need to make a call and then I'll be with you. Just stay with her. I won't be long.'

Once Auntie Loretta pulled up in her car, I explained to my brother and sister that she had phoned a doctor. He and his wife were family friends and she knew him well enough to explain what she believed was Mum's problem. As soon as she had been given his advice, she got in her car and came over. I had left the front door unlocked so that she could walk in without ringing the bell. She came into the sitting room and said hello to all of us. A wave of relief overcame me as she was now taking charge. I had really been feeling out of my depth. Mum was looking up at her but said nothing.

My aunt handed me one of the large paper bags she had brought with her. 'Be better if you three go outside for a while. It's nice and warm now and here are some fruit juices as well as some buttered scones, jam and some cakes so you can have a little picnic out there.' The word 'cakes' was enough to stop my brother and sister looking annoyed about not being able to stay in and listen to what she and Mum would be talking about. I understood that the conversation she wanted to have with her sister would not be good for them to hear – they were much too young. I would rather have stayed, even though it would be a difficult conversation, but I managed to look as though I wanted some fresh air.

'I don't know about you two, but I'm starving so let's go outside,' I said blithely.

For once, my siblings wanted to sit at the outside table and tuck in. They showed no inclination to play in the garden but then I remembered they hadn't had any breakfast. But I could tell they were distressed about Mum. My sister told me that she had no idea that, when we came back from school, Mum would look so ill – 'I knew she wasn't well, but I didn't think she would have looked so bad. I suppose I should have got hold of Dad, but I was just hoping she would get better when you were with her, Marc.'

Thank goodness she hadn't rung Steve, the very architect of what was wrong.

'Oh, don't worry, sis. Auntie Loretta will get in touch with him once she sees how Mum is,' I told her.

I could tell that they accepted that our aunt would be the best person to help Mum. We ate in silence – I think we were all wondering what Loretta's plan would be to get her youngest sister back to normality.

It took forever for our aunt to come out to us. She told us that she was going to take Mum to see a doctor. She must have called her doctor friend again, which meant she had managed to get an appointment fast. I had to tell her that

Steve didn't know about me coming over to see Mum after school. Then my sister started telling her that he hadn't been told anything about how Mum was.

'Don't worry, I can give him a ring and let him know I'm taking her to see a doctor,' Loretta told her. She then turned to me. 'Marc, are you all right about staying here with your brother and sister?'

For a few seconds I thought, bang goes my homework. Then my inner voice stepped in, ever practical. *Just explain the problem at home to the teacher who set the homework. They'll understand and give you more time to finish it. Now, Marc, just say what's right.*

'Yes, of course I will, and if it takes a long time at the doctor, I'll get us all some tea as well.'

* * *

It's one of those days in my life that has never left my mind. Even now, I'm so thankful that I made that call to Mum's sister. I think she had a pretty good idea of what was wrong with Mum when I was on the phone, especially when I told her about those short, repetitive and incomplete sentences, and the conversation with her doctor friend must have cemented her suspicions. Whatever she said to Mum while we three kids were outside, she managed to get her to agree to see the doctor.

What none of us knew then was that it was the psychiatrist who worked on a psychiatric ward that her sister was taking her to see – her doctor friend had arranged this for her.

Loretta certainly got Mum looking a bit more like herself too. Her hair was brushed and she was wearing a set of well-ironed, clean clothes. It was a relief to see her looking like that. Us three gave her hugs as she was leaving. We remained standing at the door so that we could wave to her until the car disappeared. Then we turned around and walked back into the sitting room.

Just as I was trying to relax a bit, I was bombarded with questions from my brother and sister. Who was the doctor? What would they do for Mum? When would she and Auntie come back? And what was wrong with Mum anyway? All I could tell them was that we needed to wait until the doctor had seen her and then our aunt would phone with news. We all kept looking at the clock. When the phone finally rang, Loretta told me that Mum would be staying in hospital for a while. She promised me she would call Steve and also let Gran know.

I explained to my siblings that Mum was going to stay in hospital so that she could rest for a while. I was a bit nervous about telling them, but they seemed relieved that she would be getting help. Even at their young age, they seemed to know that something was very wrong.

When my aunt arrived back, I asked her again if Mum seemed happy to stay in hospital

'Yes, Marc, being there will do her a lot of good,' she told me. 'Your mum was smiling and less confused after she had spent some time with the doctor. Now, don't worry about your dad. We've already spoken and he's on his way home.

He asked me if I could sort out what she needs at the hospital so I said I'd do that.' Turning to my sister, she said, 'Can you give me a hand?' She then asked if I would mind staying with my brother and sister until she got back again – 'It won't take me long. I only have to drop the case into the ward.'

Of course I said yes, though I was hoping she would be back before Steve – I didn't want to have to explain anything to him. She and my sister popped upstairs and soon came down carrying a large bag that looked pretty full.

'I did tell Steve that one of us would be waiting until he got here,' my aunt said tentatively.

'So, he knows I'm here?'

'Of course he does, Marc, and he said he's very grateful that you are.'

Luckily, it ended up being my aunt who had to tell Steve what had happened. I'm sure that she thought that Mum's breakdown was all his fault, not that she would have said anything like that to him. Steve arrived just as she arrived back from the hospital. To my surprise, I saw that he was really upset. He actually put his hand on my shoulder and thanked me for coming.

I felt a little relieved when my aunt said she would give me a lift back to Mum's friend Eve's house, where I was still staying. From the look Steve gave me, I knew that he was keen for me to stay, but there was no way I wanted to be in the house with him. I jumped up and picked up my school bag to indicate that I was ready to leave.

18

When I woke up the day after Mum went into hospital, I thought it would be better for me to be with Gran. I suspected that she had already been told by Loretta, her eldest daughter, that her youngest one was in hospital. I'm sure she must have felt thrown that everything had happened so quickly. I imagined her sitting downstairs, staring at the clock hands and waiting for the time when she could leave the house and visit her daughter.

Some evenings, the family would go round to Gran's home but I didn't like the thought of her being worried and alone so often, and especially now; I felt that it would not be good for her. I was a bit taken aback when, just before I left for school, Eve's phone rang and it was Gran asking to speak to me. She told me how grateful she and Auntie Loretta were for the help I had given Mum. She then asked me if I would like to stay with her while Mum was away.

'Yes, I would love to do that. Thank you, Gran,' I told her.

When we finished talking, I explained to Eve why I was going to stay with Gran. She said she understood totally and agreed that it would be good for our grandmother, who had only lost her husband a couple of years before, to have some company. She then offered to pick me up in her car and take me over to Gran's when school was over for the day – she would pack my suitcase for me and bring it with her. As a good friend of Mum's, she, too, was concerned, especially as I had already told her about the bruises and Mum's state of mind when I got in the night before.

Eve was waiting for me just outside the school in her car when we finished for the day. When I got in and she drove off, she asked me to keep in touch and to give her updates on Mum's progress. She said that she would like to know how Mum was and if she could visit her in hospital.

Once we reached Gran's, Eve patted my shoulder and said, 'Good for you, Marc, getting help for your mum and being so caring about your grandmother.'

'I'll keep in touch with you while I'm here and let you know how Mum is, I promise,' I told her.

I took my suitcase out of the boot, slammed it shut and then walked up to Gran's front door. She was waiting for me there and gave me such a nice hug. Smiling warmly at me, she said that she was so pleased I was going to stay with her, which made me feel happy.

* * *

I have already told you how my mother, with her deep depression, agreed to be admitted to hospital. What I didn't know for a long time were the details of the treatment she was having. Of course, I now know what they all were.

Every time Gran went to see Mum, she did her best to reassure me that she was beginning to get better. I knew she went over to see Mum on three different occasions while I was at school. That made me wish that I could go with her over the weekend and I was sure that Mum would be pleased to see me. I was thinking that the two of us could chat together and I would try my hardest to think of some stories that would get her laughing again. Also, I wanted to hear from her that she was feeling a lot better, which would be really good news.

When I asked Gran if I could go with her to the hospital, to my disappointment, she just told me that Mum needed to rest and I would have to wait a while.

'You could write her a letter,' she suggested, 'and I'll take it to her. She'll be so pleased to get it.'

So, I sat down and wrote to her at once, telling her that I was happy at Gran's and that Eve and I sent lots and lots of love and I so wanted to see her.

After Mum had been in the hospital for just over a week, Gran could tell just how much I wanted to go and see her. This time, she tried to explain why it was better for my mother not to have any visitors apart from her.

'It's because of the therapy she's having there, Marc. I've been told quite a lot by the head nurse of the ward she's on.

He was the one who explained why it's better for your mum not to have visitors coming who would want to chat to her.'

'Why?' I asked as I was sure that Mum's other sisters would all want to visit her there as well.

'It's because it's important that she doesn't forget what she and the therapist have been talking about,' Gran told me. 'I can remember you telling me that her memory was none too good when you were sitting with her until Loretta came over. Now I think it must be even worse. That's one of the reasons why they're trying to get that part of her mind better – I think that's why I'm the only person who can visit her for now.'

Gran went on to tell me that Mum always sat in a quiet place after her therapy session, so that she could write notes of what she wanted to talk about at her next appointment. I asked how long Mum's treatment would go on for and she kept saying, 'Just a few more weeks, Marc.' Knowing how much I was missing my mother, she kept telling me after each visit that Mum was much calmer now.

When I asked if that meant she might be coming out soon, Gran must have wished she hadn't said that. 'But, Marc, your mother still needs to be there for a little longer. Like any illness, she must be completely healed before she can leave. I know you feel it's taking a long time, but she's receiving the best treatment there. When she does come back, she'll be so much brighter,' she insisted.

The one thing Gran kept from me was that Mum was having electric-shock treatment. It sounds such a brutal, archaic thing now but it was fairly standard at the time for people in Mum's condition. She had also made it clear to the staff at the hospital that they mustn't mention anything about her treatment when I eventually visited. Evidently, it was because she thought I was too young to hear. Auntie Loretta had acted so wisely in taking Mum to the psychiatrist and he was best placed to get her well again.

When Mum's sisters came over to see us, it was clear from the tone of the conversation that they were against her going back to Steve ever again. It seemed to me that, apart from Loretta and Gran, they had a knack of asking me questions. One was why hadn't I gone back home with Mum after those three weeks she had stayed away from Steve and then decided to go back? I felt that they were annoyed that I hadn't been loyal to her. Hiding my annoyance, I somehow managed a smile before telling them my reasons for not wanting to be in a house with Steve. I said that he would be fine for a while until that temper of his came back and then our lives would be hell all over again. He was always having a go at me and his constant snapping and shouting made it almost impossible for me to finish my homework.

They nodded and then my Auntie said, 'Oh, I can see why that would be a problem for you. I never thought he treated you like his own kids.'

The talk about Mum and Steve carried on and it became clear that they all thought that he was a danger. 'Thank goodness he can't visit her in the hospital – well, none of us can except Mum. Glad he's not there to upset her,' said Loretta.

She then repeated how Mum needed to rest a lot,

which was why only Gran could visit her. It was clear they understood and wanted to protect her.

I have never forgotten that heartbreaking day when, after listening to my little brother, I had gone over to my mother's house to see what was wrong with her. I had sat with Mum and listened to her confused speech, which told me she was getting much worse. I believed then, as I still do now, that from what she kept telling me, she felt trapped in a life that she no longer wanted to be a part of.

It was hard to know what to say and I felt completely helpless.

19

Being only 13, I did my best to understand why I wasn't able to visit my mother. *It's for the sake of her health and that's what's important, isn't it?* I kept telling myself, but I became increasingly anxious despite Gran's reassurances.

'So, Steve still can't visit either?' I asked my grandmother when we were having tea together one day.

'No, he can't. She doesn't want him there and neither does her doctor. The staff have all been told there's a ban on her husband visiting. I told the sister that it was Steve who had given her those bruises. I've gone over it in my head again and again and I think all those rows caused her to have a breakdown. You knew about them, didn't you, Marc?' she said.

'Yes, there were so many rows. That's why I couldn't stand being there anymore,' I told her.

'I had already realised that, Marc, which is why I told the nurse all about you not wanting to stay in your home. He reassured me that Steve wouldn't be allowed in to see her.

He also said that they didn't want any more bad memories or fears being foremost in her mind right now.

'I hope you feel all right being here and seeing your aunts come over and talking away as they do,' she said hesitantly.

'Yes, Gran, of course I feel fine about being here and I love seeing them in the evenings too. I'd like to spend more time with my little brother and sister, although I manage to see them at school. They're both missing Mum badly. It was my brother who told me that she wasn't well and asked me to go with them when school finished.'

'Thank goodness you did, Marc – you couldn't have handled it any better,' she said gratefully. I could tell from her expression that she thought that Mum would have got far worse if I hadn't seen her for myself and made that phone call. I felt proud that I could finally make a difference in Mum's life after feeling so helpless before.

'I bet you're the person your mum's really missing now,' Gran said suddenly, which made us both smile.

After that conversation, I still couldn't help but wonder how long it would be before I saw my mother again. Gran did tell me that one time when she visited, Mum had looked relieved when she told her that I made sure to spend time with my little brother and sister during break time at school. I always insisted my siblings seemed to be all right, although that was not strictly true – they were worried about both their parents. At break times, my brother kept coming over to find me. He so wanted me to walk back home after school with them and stay there.

'Dad seems really miserable,' he kept telling me. 'He's got a cleaner to come in once a week but that's all she does. Dad just buys ready meals or takeaways. It's not like Mum's food.'

One day, just before the bell rang to signal our break was over, my brother came out with an important question: 'When will she be coming home? Do you know, Marc?'

But I couldn't tell him then how long it would be before Mum had recovered sufficiently to be discharged from hospital. Gran had told me about her not wanting to see Steve and it made me wonder if that was the reason why he was so unhappy. I still had a picture in my head of what happened when he came home after my aunt had taken her to hospital. He had looked very upset then and I remember that he didn't want me to leave. Then I stopped feeling sorry for him because I kept seeing Mum's bruises in my mind. I knew all her family, myself included, wanted her to keep away from him, though I couldn't help but wonder how my brother and sister would feel if she didn't come home the day she came out of hospital.

That was when I came up with the idea that it should be Gran's house she would come to stay in, at least for a while. I could bring my siblings back there after school to see her and even help them with their homework when they were there. It was a bit of a dream, I suppose – my stepdad would hardly be pleased about Mum being at Gran's house and those two visiting her there. Still, as he seemed to love them, maybe he would put them first.

As more weeks went by, Mum remained in hospital and I found it hard to suppress my longing to visit her, especially because I was free at weekends. However, after Gran's explanation of why it was better for Mum not to have visitors, I forced myself to accept that I wasn't going to be visiting just yet, although it really wasn't easy for me to do this.

At my young age, I really didn't know much about psychiatric hospitals. The question in my mind was, how did the patients spend their days while they were in there? It must be so dull, I thought. Realising this was puzzling me, Gran tried her best to explain what they were like.

'I wish I could take photos so that you could see it for yourself, but that's not allowed. I can tell you, though, that the ward your mum is on is very different to the hospitals you might imagine.'

'So, what's it like then?' I asked nervously.

'There are two wards with beds: one for men and the other for women. In the middle of them, there's a big comfy sitting room where they can spend time during the day, reading or writing to friends. There's lots of space and they can watch TV in the early evenings. Once or twice a week, someone comes round with books, which can be borrowed. Some people just talk or play cards and the ones who don't want company often just stare out of the window. There's also a café up on another floor. People visiting their relatives can take them up there so they can enjoy a coffee and get out of the ward for a while.'

She told me then that Mum often rested on her bed with

a book – 'Though after her tea, she might join the other patients to watch something on TV.'

'So, it's not much different from being at home?' I asked hopefully.

'Only there's no cleaning, no washing, no ironing or cooking, or tidying up after the family!' Gran laughed.

'I guess it's more enjoyable in there then than being at home,' I said wryly.

That made Gran smile a little. I think she could tell that I felt more relaxed now. I suppose then I hadn't really understood why Mum was in hospital for so long. Some of my friends' mums had been in hospital for operations or to have babies. Their kids could visit just about every day until they came home in a few days, or on one occasion, a couple of weeks. No wonder I was surprised that my mum was away so long.

Depression and anxiety also cause forgetfulness and that takes a lot longer to heal.

20

I was increasingly aware that Gran and Mum's sisters wanted to make sure that she didn't go back to Steve. From what they were saying, I could tell that they were concerned about my little brother and sister too. 'They must be wishing that she'll be back soon,' said one of my aunts. 'I can't think what will happen to them when she doesn't return to their home.

'It can't be good for those two, living with their father,' another chimed in.

Hearing this, I interjected, 'There's no need to be worried about my brother and sister being alone with their father. He's never bad-tempered with them. Nothing's too much trouble for his own kids. My brother does miss her, though. He keeps asking me when she'll be back.

'The other day, I almost bumped into Steve when he was collecting them from school. I think he must have been taking them out to a café for their tea.'

'So why didn't he ask you to go as well?' one of my aunts said.

Before I could answer that, Aunt Loretta said, 'From what you've told us, he's not that nice to you.'

'Maybe because I'm not his son,' I said. 'I know he adopted me when I was a baby, but I suppose that was only to help Mum.'

There was a sudden deathly silence – unusual for Mum's sisters. They must have known who my real father was and I was tired of them all pretending that Steve was my real father. More than that, I wanted to tell them what Mum had said that had made her so tearful when I was alone with her that day and had caused me to phone Auntie Loretta.

Before I could say anything, Gran asked me if I knew about my dad.

I took a deep breath and then I said that I knew that I had a different father to my siblings, 'Mum never told me anything about him, nor did Steve. It was me who found out a long time ago. I found some papers in a cupboard with some names on them and so I pulled them out. When I read what was printed there, I knew Steve was not my father and that my real one was dead.'

I didn't tell them about my visit to my uncle, who had explained much of what happened just after I had been born. I only said that I knew I shouldn't have been looking in the cupboard, but I was curious.

I could tell from their faces that they were shocked by what I had just told them.

'Oh, don't worry about me,' I quickly added. 'Of course, I'm sad my real father isn't here but I'm pleased that Steve's not my dad. I'm sure none of you would want me taking after him, would you?'

Their nervous laughter broke the tension in the room.

One of Mum's sisters had mentioned earlier that Mum had a therapist in the hospital to whom she was able to talk about her problems.

'Do you know what they talk about?' I asked curiously.

'No, not really. Anyhow, that's all meant to be confidential,' I was told.

It was then that I felt that I had to let them know that I knew my real father had committed suicide and it was Mum's memory of him and how he had killed himself that she had talked about that day when I phoned Loretta – 'She kept telling me that she blamed herself a lot for him committing suicide and telling me about her memories of him. I expect she's been talking to the therapist about that because that's what she kept telling me, repeating it over and over.'

I looked up and met Loretta's eyes. There was no surprise in them. She just smiled at me hesitantly and so I went on.

'It was very clear to me that day when I sat close to Mum that she felt so guilty about what happened. That must be why she never goes to see anyone in Dad's family, though one of his cousins came to see her and invited her over. But she never did go.

'She must have known them quite well when she was living with Dad. As I sat beside her waiting for Auntie Loretta to come, all those memories of him kept coming out. I could tell she was miserable and that's what was getting me so scared.'

I did my best not to cry but it took some effort.

Auntie Loretta spoke to me gently as she drew me to her to comfort me. The others nodded and I could feel their love and support.

Having told them all this, I felt exhausted and unable to say much more. However, they continued with their conversation, repeating how they didn't want Mum going back to Steve.

Another aunt said, 'If only she hadn't gone back to Steve the last time. Maybe then she might have been all right.'

'Still, she's an adult,' Loretta insisted. 'We can try our best, but if we can't make her stay away from him, there's nothing we can do.'

Another aunt pointed out that there was another problem: 'I mean, which of the parents would have the other two children?'

I didn't bother telling them that I knew Steve's daughter would protest strongly if she wasn't allowed to live with her dad.

'It's the law that sorts that out when it comes to divorce,' said Loretta firmly and she finally got up to leave. Thankfully, the other sisters did the same – I could tell Gran was tired and needed to rest. I don't think either of us could take any more.

Once they had all gone, Gran and I sat down together over a cup of tea and we both said that we were looking forward to Mum coming out. Then she kissed me on the forehead and we went upstairs to bed.

21

There I was, thinking I was finally going with Gran to the hospital at the weekend to see Mum. I had been so pleased when she said that I could go with her.

'Your mother's so much calmer now, Marc,' she told me when I asked how Mum was. 'When she heard that you were so wanting to come with me, she said she couldn't wait to see you again.'

Full of anticipation, I was expecting to go with Gran after school the next day. I was so relieved that my mum was getting better and the day dragged as I waited for the time of our visit to come. But on the Wednesday when I came back from school and as I reached Gran's house, I saw that my gran stood waiting for me at the door. Even though I was still a few yards away, I could tell that she was looking remarkably happy. *Must be something good about Mum*, I thought to myself as I walked up to her. The moment I came close to Gran, her arms flew around me. She gave me such a huge hug that it made me think she must have some really good news. Before I could ask, she said, 'Come on into the sitting room. I'll be with you as soon as I've made us some tea. I have news!'

'What is it you want tell me?' I said eagerly.

'Oh, you'll know soon enough,' she said mysteriously as she bustled into the kitchen.

I was so curious about what it could be but in no doubt it would be something that would make me feel really cheerful too. After dropping my satchel against the wall by the kitchen – I certainly wasn't going to look at my books – I went into the sitting room to wait for Gran to bring tea and explain what was going on.

I always worked as fast as I could on my homework so that I could get it done before all or some of Mum's sisters arrived. *It can wait, I'll do it later*, I told myself. After all, it usually took about an hour and a half and my aunts wouldn't mind if I was still scribbling away in the kitchen while they sat chatting in the sitting room.

Having not seen Gran in such a happy state, not long after she must have come from the hospital, I was dying to find out what had happened there. A few minutes later, she came in carrying a tray with tea and biscuits.

'I've got some really good news for you,' she announced as she placed our cup and saucers in front of us. Before I could ask anything, she said, 'It's settled, Marc. You won't be coming to the hospital with me at the weekend. Now don't look upset. Your mum's been told that she's well enough to leave there. The really good news is that she'll be coming straight here tomorrow to stay with us.'

I was so surprised that I almost spilt my tea all over the light cream carpet.

'You mean she's out of hospital for good now?' I spluttered.

'More or less, but she'll have to go there twice a week to see her therapist. That means she'll be what's known as an outpatient by tomorrow. While I was there, I met her doctor and he was so pleased that her mental state has finally recovered enough for her to leave. He also said that one of the staff will bring her over tomorrow. I know I could go there and bring her back myself, but he wanted to make it as easy as he could. The head nurse sorted out someone to bring her back here and, as I was saying goodbye to them, he smiled at me and said at least I would have time to sort out a bedroom for her.'

I couldn't believe that Mum was at last coming back and I felt so excited that I couldn't stop myself from saying, 'You mean she's coming here tomorrow?'

'That's right,' said Gran, smiling.

'What time will she be here, will I be back from school?'

'About half eleven, definitely before lunchtime. And before you ask any more questions, she'll be staying here for a while.'

That made me feel overjoyed, for I would be able to spend lots of time with her as we would be living in the same place again. Gran hadn't said just how long she would be staying there, though. Perhaps it was because Mum didn't know how long she would have to keep seeing her therapist, and anyway, she would need to relax afterwards. So many questions were churning through my head.

After pouring more tea for us, Gran told me that she was going out early in the morning to make sure there was plenty of good food in the house before Mum arrived. 'I'll get all her favourites,' she said with an indulgent smile. I could tell that she was just as pleased as I was about my mother being well enough to come and stay with us, although I sort of guessed that she might want to live in a place of her own later on and then she could have her friends over whenever she wanted. Mum must have been hoping that her two other children would be coming to stay with her often too. Of course, back then I didn't have a clue about what she could afford or how much her income would be. Also, I knew nothing about benefits or how the council could find a home for her. In fact, there was another question floating in my mind which bothered me: how would Mum be able to spend time with her two young ones without Steve being there with them?

So long as she didn't go back to him ...

I thought she could meet them at school, but then Steve would know she was out of hospital as my sister would find it hard not to tell him straight away that she had seen Mum. Knowing Gran as well as I did, I was pretty sure that she already knew what Mum's plan was; a plan that she wasn't about to share with me at this stage.

Just enjoy seeing your mum again, my inner voice said.

I knew all of Mum's family really hoped that Steve was

out of her life forever but I couldn't see how that was possible when they had children together and that really bothered me. Try as I might, I kept thinking about my brother and sister and how they wanted Mum to come back to their house. I decided that I mustn't let them know that she was coming out of hospital that week. Anyway, Gran hadn't said anything about them to me.

It's up to Mum to work out how she'll spend time with them, not me, I kept telling myself. But I couldn't help but feel worried about us all.

* * *

During breaks the next day at school, I stayed inside most of the time – I just didn't want to see my siblings or face a barrage of questions. Lying to them was not something I wanted to do, so avoidance seemed the best option. Keeping out of their way made me feel rather mean. I was sure that my little brother had no idea that Mum was coming out of the hospital.

Be sensible. It's up to the grown-ups and not you, came that nagging inner voice again. Still, I couldn't stop myself from feeling excited about seeing Mum again as soon as I could get out of school. I kept wishing that I could have taken the day off to be with her the moment she arrived. Knowing Gran, this was something she wouldn't have agreed to but at least I would get to spend the rest of the day and evening with my mother. A contented smile crept onto my face.

I didn't know that a disappointment would be coming

my way later on – a disappointment that also would affect Mum's sisters as well as Gran. In school, all I could think about was seeing Mum again and I don't think I learned a thing that day. I kept imagining us sitting together, catching up. Would she want to talk much, or would she be distant? I had to be prepared for all possibilities.

During the lunch break, I suddenly remembered that I had homework to do. I groaned aloud at the thought – I knew it would take at least an hour, or even more.

Get permission to put it aside until the weekend, said that inner voice of mine.

It was just after the final bell rang, indicating classes were over, when I managed to catch my maths teacher coming out of another classroom. Luckily, I knew which room he would be teaching in. I liked him a lot because he was always encouraging so I hoped he'd be understanding. Luckily, he was.

'Your mother's been ill for a long time, so of course, you must be thrilled that she's well enough to come home,' he said kindly.

'I am,' I told him.

'Marc, you're not to worry about your homework,' he said with a friendly smile. 'You can give it to me before the end of next week so go ahead and have a good time with your mother. I'm sure you couldn't even think about getting it right today. There are just too many other things going round in your head right now. They must be much more important to you than your maths.'

I thanked him profusely.

'Your mother must also be looking forward to seeing you, so best be off now so you can get home as fast as you can.'

I repeated my thanks and sped off, hoping there was no chance of me bumping into my little brother. Gran's house was about three quarters of a mile away. Halfway there, I was panting.

Mum must have been looking out of the window for me. Once she saw me, she came out and stood at the top of the path, waiting for me. I was so happy that I almost danced on my toes when I got closer. I threw my arms around her and gave her a gentle hug, just in case she was still bruised from Steve's fists. She wrapped her arms around me tightly and almost lifted me off my feet.

'Oh, Marc, I've missed you so much,' she said tearfully.

'And me you,' I said as we walked into the sitting room with our arms still linked and sat down on the sofa. 'Where's Gran?' I added.

'Sorting out a few things upstairs,' she said. 'I think that's her excuse so that we can really catch up.'

And we didn't stop talking. The questions came flooding out of me, such as, what was it like in the hospital? Mum told me that, during her time there, she had been given a great deal of help from just about everyone. 'That finally got me thinking clearly again,' she said. 'As you know, I was all over the place. But, Marc, I think the treatment got me back to my old self.'

Hearing this came as a huge relief. Of course, I had been

wondering if, after being in hospital for such a long time, my mother would be the same as she was before what Aunt Loretta had said was a breakdown. At that age, I still didn't understand exactly how a breakdown could finally go away, but I know now.

I also wanted to know what the other patients on the ward were like. Mum thought about this for a moment and then she told me that the other women were all pleasant and helpful. They had group therapy but also achieved a lot when they shared their stories more informally in the lounge. Still curious, I kept on with my questions and she told me more about her experiences in hospital.

'There were a couple of women in there that I got really friendly with. One had such a sad story, though. I felt so sorry for her – her parents were nothing like mine, who were always kind to my sisters and me. This particular woman told me that her mother hadn't wanted a child, especially a daughter. Once she was at school and heard what the other girls' mothers were like, she became aware that her own mum scarcely had time for her. There were no birthday parties or special party dresses for her. When it came to her birthday, she was given a school uniform, not nice toys. She was never taken out to the playground or the park, let alone an ice-cream shop. It was only when her grandmother came visiting that she was hugged and kissed and taken to a café for tea and cakes and bought presents.'

'Was that why she was in the hospital, Mum?'

'Partly, I suppose. She told me that if children don't have

love, once they get older, they long for it. By the time they are well into their teens, they search for it, hoping they will find someone to care for them. Unfortunately, it's often the wrong people that they become involved with. Being desperate for affection meant she had too many relationships with the wrong young men. She even went out with a much older man. She believed he loved her, but she was wrong. They were together for a couple of years and he just wanted to control her. There were other mistakes after him. No wonder she was in hospital. Her last boyfriend made fun of her and made her feel plain, inadequate and stupid. But she was so beautiful, Marc.'

That made me gasp. How could anyone be so cruel?

'There are all sorts of reasons why someone's life goes wrong,' Mum explained. 'It was this women's honesty when we were together that really got to me. Most of us talked about why we had ended up on the ward. We listened to each other and, as we healed inside, we became more confident and helped each other by being supportive and encouraging.'

From what Mum was telling me, it was clear so many of these women had experienced such sad lives. I felt so sorry for them, but I also admired the staff who did their best to help the patients. When I asked if that included her, Mum said, 'They did, indeed. All of us were determined that we would never need to be placed in that sort of hospital again but we had to accept that it was down to us to sort out our lives. You might say we needed to fight for it. Once we decided how we wanted our future to be, we made plans.

If we stick to them and don't let anyone change our minds, then the rest of our lives will be much calmer and happier.'

As she finished telling me this, I began to feel more confident about her future. From what she said, it meant that she would refuse to allow anyone to muddle up her memories again. I had seen how both anxiety and distress had preyed on her mind that day when I rang my aunt for help. I never wanted to see that again for I loved my mother dearly and wanted her to be calm and contented for the rest of her life.

22

When I came into the sitting room with Mum, a large pot of tea was already set out with slices of cake that Gran must have baked for us. Mum topped up our cups a few times as we continued talking. She didn't once mention Steve, which rather shocked me when I looked back on that whole conversation. She did ask after my brother and sister, though, so I told her how I had spent time with them at school on our breaks. I could hardly say how eager they were to see her. Instead, I told her that they were getting on well at school.

We must have been chatting for at least an hour when Mum told me a little about her therapist that Gran had also mentioned to me. I didn't ask what they had talked about. I certainly had no intention of reminding her of that day she went into hospital; a day no doubt she had described to the therapist.

Mum must have guessed what was on my mind for she smiled and said, 'I know you're not going to say anything about that afternoon you had to telephone Loretta. But now, thanks to my therapist, I have stopped being scared to talk about your real dad with you and I won't stop you from seeing his family. Don't worry about how you found out about him. I should have told you all this a long time ago but there never seemed to be a good moment. I can remember what I kept saying to you that day. I couldn't stop telling you all about him, but you didn't ask any questions – I think you must have been just too worried about me. It was as I told my therapist about it that I realised that you must already know about your dad and what happened. When Gran came in after that particular session, I had already worked out what you knew. I asked if she had any idea how that might have happened. She told me about you looking in the cupboard and how you found all that paperwork. So, Marc, I know you did your own investigation – quite the young detective, you are!'

She shot me an amused glance, which caused me to blush. We both burst out laughing.

It was then that we began to talk more about my brother and sister. I felt comfortable telling her everything I knew about how they were doing. I also mentioned that my stepfather often turned up at school to take them out.

'Did he never ask for you to go with them?' she wanted to know.

'No, but then he wasn't looking for me and I kept well out of his way,' I said. 'Even so, they miss you a lot. I know that because my brother especially keeps asking questions about you. Where are you and why can't he visit? You know the sort of thing.'

I didn't tell her that he also wanted to know when she would be home. It was hardly the moment to ask when she had planned to spend more time with them.

Gran suddenly appeared at the door. Before I said anything else about my siblings, she asked if I could give her a hand in the kitchen.

'Not you, dear,' she told my mother, who had started to get up. 'You just stay here and relax. Marc and I will bring you in some fresh tea and more of that cake for the three of us to enjoy.'

'Well, I wouldn't mind another piece – it's so nice,' said Mum.

Gran smiled indulgently at her daughter as I got up to go in the kitchen with her.

My grandmother had her reasons for getting me out of the sitting room and into the kitchen. It didn't take long before she said very quietly that there was something she had to tell me without Mum hearing. I should have guessed that she had an ulterior motive. Almost every secret I have ever heard has a knack of coming out in the kitchen! Gran said that she hadn't wanted me to get annoyed or upset in front of my mother. In fact, her first few words were, 'Don't get upset, Marc.' The next ones were, 'Steve's coming over to see her.' Funnily enough, I was hardly surprised. I can't say I was pleased, but at least I wasn't too upset – I just wished they had arranged this a day later so that I could have spent the whole evening with Mum.

'To be fair, Gran, I've talked a lot with my little brother and, sometimes, my sister as well. They've both been missing Mum a lot. I expect that's why Steve's coming to see her – he probably wants to talk to her about them. I'm pretty sure that after this evening, he'll want to bring them over or even take her out to meet up with them, but for the first time ever, he'll need Mum's and your permission.'

Gran smiled before saying, 'I'm just thankful you're not in a bad mood after what I've told you.'

'Well, I'm not,' I insisted. 'But, Gran, do you know if he ever visited her in hospital? I know you said they wouldn't let him in, but how did he learn that she was out now? It had to be her or one of the nurses who told him when she was leaving.'

'He must have visited her, I suppose,' she told me. 'I didn't ask but the head nurse must have decided she was ready to see him and approved the visit.'

'Mmm,' I said, 'of course, she had her phone with her. That's why he must have known when you weren't going over, so that he could visit on those evenings.'

'Ah,' said my grandmother, 'of course, I wouldn't expect him to turn up when I was there.'

'Now, don't worry about me getting upset, Gran, although I'm sure my aunts will be annoyed when they know about it.'

'Oh, don't say that, Marc. I was worried about that too! I messaged them to say he was coming and they're not at all happy.'

'So, they're not coming over this evening?'

'No, none of them are.'

'But the kids will be so pleased about her being back, Gran. When they hear they're coming over to see Mum later on, they'll be over the moon.'

'Well, I hope so, Marc.'

I did my best to stop Gran worrying about my stepfather coming over, especially as neither Mum's sisters nor her friends would be able to visit until there was an evening without him or my siblings being there. I could understand that as I didn't want to see him, so neither would they. Of course, they would be upset that he was going to be at Gran's on the very first day Mum had arrived and Gran and I would have much preferred having all my aunts and a few of mother's friends filling up the sitting room on her first day back – it would have been such a great evening. Mum's sisters were a lot of fun and I knew that they wouldn't have been able to stop themselves telling lots of stories until the room was filled with laughter.

That inner voice of mine told me that, for Mum and Gran's sake, I would have to be polite to my stepfather once he was here. While we had been talking, Gran had set the kettle on to boil and the tea was made. More cake was sliced and we put butter and jam on a plate of homemade scones. I carried the tray into the sitting room and placed it on the small table in front of Mum before telling her, 'I'd best get some homework done, but I'll take some more tea and cake with me.'

I felt that I should let Gran tell her daughter that I knew about Steve coming. I suspected Mum would be a bit embarrassed that she hadn't managed to tell me herself.

23

So, what did I feel when my stepfather arrived at the house? Nothing much is the answer. I think I must have ignored my homework as I decided to get nicely dressed and to make sure I could put a friendly smile on my face when I saw him. After all, Mum had only just come out of hospital and I wanted her to feel all right about his visit. Or should I say that she must have hoped that Gran and I were none too disappointed in her for agreeing to have Steve over.

Soon came the knock on the door.

'That will be Steve. Shall I go to the door and let him in?' Mum asked Gran tentatively.

'Yes, of course, dear,' she told her.

I had come down to the sitting room to wait for his arrival. When we heard them coming in, Gran and I stood up to greet him. I noticed straight away that he was carrying a large bunch of beautiful flowers, which he handed to Gran.

'I know you like flowers,' he said with a warm, friendly

smile. 'When I saw them in the florist's, I couldn't resist getting them for you.'

Of course, Gran thanked him before she went out to put them in water.

'I'll be putting them out in vases later on,' she said when she came back. 'They're really lovely. It's so nice of you to remember how much I love them and especially those colours too.'

I could tell from her face that Mum was happy that Steve was there. *Did she still want to be with him?* I tried to push that thought away, especially after what she had already told me about the future.

For a short time, we sat together and chatted a little, although nothing more was said about Mum's time in hospital. I had noticed how good my mother was looking when I first saw her and I wondered if Steve was noticing too. The expression on his face did tell me that he still cared for her, but then he shouldn't have lost his temper so often. I think that he knew I had never forgotten his rows with Mum. I couldn't believe it when he turned to me and said, 'Marc, I owe you an apology. I'm really sorry I was often so nasty to you. I know there's no excuse but all those strikes and closures sent me mad.'

I could understand what he was trying to say, but then why did he behave so differently with his own children? There was a lot of depression in the town, I knew – friends experienced upsets in their families when jobs were lost and there was a lack of money to boot. When I mentioned that, Steve sighed and said, 'You're right there. Another big problem is that so many husbands aren't with their families so much because some have been forced to find jobs elsewhere. This town has turned into a far less happy place.'

'Let's hope it will change later on as new businesses come here,' I said.

Steve, Mum and Gran nodded in agreement.

I was somewhat grateful that Steve had admitted to being depressed and in a bad temper when the town's difficulties first rose. It was listening to him that made me remember how good he had been to me after my weeks of potato picking. The memory of this made me warm towards him and I couldn't help smiling at him.

Gran suddenly interjected, 'I know you were one of the men in charge of some of those strikes, but by the end of them, it was distressing for everyone.'

There was a pause before the subject was changed.

It was about an hour later, after all of us had had enough to eat and were awash with tea, when Gran asked me to come with her for a little stroll.

'It does my old legs good,' she told Mum and Steve.

'Yes, Gran, of course I'll come with you,' I said.

I suppose we both felt it was better leaving them for a while so that they could talk about my brother and sister. I think we were hoping that it was only their family that had made him come over.

The walk was quite long and, tough as she was, I began to notice that Gran was beginning to look tired.

'Maybe we should start walking home now,' I suggested and, thankfully, she agreed.

Once back, we found the two of them sitting quite close to each other and Mum looked calm. As for Steve, he must have really sold the good part of himself and promised that she would be well looked after if she went back, or so I suspected.

Steve left fairly soon after that, after thanking Gran for allowing him to come over. His goodbye to me seemed genuine and he also seemed grateful that I had been almost friendly towards him.

It was when I went to school on the day after Steve's visit that I saw my siblings standing near the gate with him. I wondered what that was about but we didn't have much time to talk before classes began.

'Morning, Marc,' said Steve, greeting me with one of his pleasant smiles as soon as I came close.

I was glad to see that both my siblings were looking so happy so I had to smile back.

'We're seeing Mum today when school's over!' said my little brother, jumping down with glee.

'We can hardly wait, Marc!' my sister added. 'You're so lucky that you've already spent some time with her. What's she like now? I mean, is she very different to when she left home?'

'Hey, I already told you she's looking great,' said Steve, patting her on the shoulder. He gave me a surprisingly conspiratorial wink.

'That's right,' I agreed. 'She's much better now and she's looking forward to spending time with you both.'

Out of the corner of my eye, I saw my stepfather glance at me, which made me think that, most probably, my sister had complained about him going to Gran's without them. And I was right for she began saying, 'Why didn't you tell us yesterday that Mum was well enough to come out of hospital?'

'She came over to Gran's after I had left for school so I didn't even know she was coming out of hospital until I got home,' I explained.

'Well, then, if she was missing us as much as Dad says, why didn't she come to our house instead of going to Gran's?' my sister said boldly.

'It's because she still has to rest a lot and Gran's near the hospital and Mum's still a day patient. Also, with Gran being in nearly all the time, she can really look after her, that's why,' I said patiently.

'You sound like a lawyer!' said Steve, placing a hand on his daughter's shoulder. He told her to 'stop asking stupid questions'. I'm sure he knew that I hadn't told her the entire truth, but he wasn't about to say anything. In fact, he looked a bit amused about this line of interrogation.

'Now, what else do you want to know?' I said to my sister, almost exasperatedly.

'Dad told us that we're going to see her over the weekend as well as today,' she told me.

'Good,' I managed to say. 'Think you'll both have a lovely time with her.'

I can't say that I thought it was good at all. Of course, Mum's sisters would be pleased about her spending time with her kids, but not with Steve there as well. And certainly not in our former home.

The day before, Gran had been really upset when she had to tell her daughters that Steve was coming over. They had all been annoyed and more than likely hurt as well. If they found out that Mum was also seeing him that afternoon, they would hardly be pleased. And even more disappointed if they knew about her seeing him again at the weekend.

I felt rather uneasy about this too. The only excuse that Mum would be able to give was that she hadn't yet arranged to take my brother and sister out on their own and, since she had been in hospital for so long, she had been missing us all.

As I was thinking of an excuse that might work, Steve said, 'Marc, we'll be picking up your mother this afternoon and then we'll go to a nice café for a late lunch or tea. Of course, I invited your gran to join us as well.'

'So, is she coming too?' I asked.

'No, she's not. She thanked me for asking, but then told me she had some baking to do. All her daughters are coming this evening and they're so looking forward to seeing their youngest sister. Now, Marc, how about you coming with us too? They have some really good burgers and cakes at the café and I'm sure your mum wants you to be there.'

In a way, I would have liked to go with them but then I thought about my grandmother. 'I think I'll need to help Gran when I get back,' I said. 'I expect she's gone shopping with Mum and they'll have brought back all the food that needs preparing. She might need some help before my aunts arrive.'

'OK then, another time.'

Luckily, as soon as Steve said this, the bell rang. The three of us sped off to our respective parts of the school.

I wondered what her sisters would say if they saw Steve bringing Mum back to Gran's. I just hoped that she would get back before they all arrived or I would be worrying about what might happen. I didn't think there would be any more surprises coming but I was completely wrong there because, when my siblings and I met up again during the lunch break, my little brother told me something that completely startled me.

'Dad's looking at another house,' he said.

'Where is it?' I wanted to know.

'About four streets away. I think he's going to take it. He asked us if we liked it and we both said yes.'

'What's it like then?'

'It's the same size as ours, but there's a larger garden.'

I wondered why Steve was looking at another house. There must be a reason and I was curious as to what that might be. No doubt he hadn't wanted me to hear about it yet. I decided that I wasn't going to say anything either.

* * *

As I walked to the gate once school was finished for the day, I noticed my brother and sister were not far behind me. They came running to the gate and I saw Steve with Mum beside him waiting in the car. Mum got out and hugged and kissed her youngest children and opened the door for the two of them to get in. Once they were sitting comfortably in the back and had their seatbelts on, she came over to me and gave me a big smile.

'Don't you worry about us going to the café. Steve will get me back well before my sisters arrive.'

I managed a smile. That certainly came as a relief.

Steve had pulled the window down and, as Mum was about to get in, he called out that he could give me a lift to Gran's.

'Thanks, I'm good,' I said, adding that it didn't take me long to get there and I actually liked the walk.

Mum turned her head and smiled at me. I think she knew that I wanted them in the café as fast as possible so she could get back in plenty of time.

I strode back fast and asked Gran what I could do to help. She gave me the job of making plates of sandwiches, while she prodded the cake with a skewer to see if it was ready for icing. A large and delicious-looking chocolate cake stood on a baking rack, cooling down.

'I finished baking the cake some time ago, Marc,' she told me. 'It needs to sit there for a while before I can ice it. Now, let's sit down for a bit and have some tea. I'm bushed! Then I'll start on the scones. The cream's whipped and in the fridge.'

Gran had already made some tea for us and put some snacks out for me too in case I was peckish and couldn't wait for teatime. Then she iced the cake while I helped get the kitchen tidy. About an hour before my aunts were due, we popped upstairs to tidy ourselves. I guessed that Gran needed a bit of a rest on her bed upstairs, especially after all the baking she had done.

Combing my hair and changing my clothes didn't seem to take long. It was a bit later when I glanced at my watch and, seeing the time, I knew that Mum would be back soon. As it was still quite warm, I sat on the bench outside the front door so that I could wait for her there.

Pure luck, but as I sat down, I saw Steve's car coming up the lane. *Thank goodness,* I said to myself. *Mum's sisters won't be here for at least half an hour.* I wondered if my siblings would get out of the car and run into Gran's house so that they could also see her because, of course, she would be delighted to see them. Even so, I didn't want them being around when our visitors arrived.

As soon as the car stopped, Mum jumped out and Steve began to turn it round. The two in the back were waving at us and Mum and I happily waved back. She looked as though she had enjoyed herself.

'I'll go upstairs for a bit,' she said. 'My make-up needs re-doing – those little ones hugged and kissed it all off!'

That made me laugh a little because she still looked good to me.

It didn't seem to take her long to put on some make-up as well as changing her clothes and she came down wearing a nice blue dress. She was looking bright-eyed and happy. Gran also came down, now looking less tired than when she went to her room.

It was only about a quarter of an hour later when I heard a couple of cars coming up the lane, which told us that Mum's sisters were arriving. Gran suggested Mum take them into the sitting room.

'I'll make some tea and Marc will help bringing it in.'

Mum stood by the door as all four sisters came in, exclaiming loudly about how pleased they were to see her. Lots of hugs followed before they went into the sitting room to catch up.

I had become quite good at carrying trays by then! Mine had the tea and sandwiches on it, while Gran brought in plates and cups. I returned to collect the cake and Gran popped the scones in the oven to warm while the kettle boiled. Once we were all in the room together and the tea was being poured, I heard the sisters say they had presents for Mum. With chuckles and smiles, small gifts were passed to her. She protested that it wasn't her birthday or Christmas, but you could see she was delighted.

I watched as she opened them with a wide smile on her face. I can't remember what all of them were, but I do recall a lovely deep-pink scarf that came from Auntie Loretta – I remember thinking it was quite beautiful. Mum looked almost as pink as her scarf when the jokes began to come out. Lots of them, in fact, that got us all laughing so hard, we almost forgot about the tea. Gran kept urging us to eat and I decided to tuck in while I watched Mum looking so happy surrounded by her family.

Nothing was said about Steve, which no doubt would

have made everyone feel awkward. They did ask after my siblings, though.

'I expect you've loved seeing them,' Auntie Loretta said.

My ears pricked up as I realised she was letting her other sisters know my mother had been with them. Mum was smart enough not to include Steve's name when she was telling them all about seeing them.

I heard her say, 'They were both so excited and came tearing out of the gate the moment school was over. When I told them about the café that I was taking them to, they were jumping up and down with excitement. They loved the cakes, but I knew you were baking, Mum, so I just had tea.' She smiled at Gran as she said this. 'My nosey little daughter kept asking about the hospital but, of course, there was a lot that I didn't want to mention. Instead, I told them what we did when Mum visited and how we had to go up to another floor to the café where we could drink tea and talk. I also explained about our sitting room and how we could watch TV in the evenings.'

'What did they say to all that?' Auntie Loretta asked curiously.

'That got them looking a bit surprised. They seemed to think that we spent all our time in bed because that's what people do in hospital on TV!'

That got the aunts laughing.

More tea was drunk, sandwiches, cake and scones consumed, but the laughter and chatter never ceased.

It was a really fun evening.

24

When I woke the next morning after that lovely evening, I went downstairs and found Mum in the kitchen, filling a glass with water. Gran wasn't about, so I seized the opportunity to ask her about the new house Steve had been looking at.

'Did you know anything about it, Mum?'

'Yes, Steve told me all about it,' she said. 'It's because there's something to do with the rent going up on our place that doesn't please him. Anyhow, he thinks the other house with the larger garden and the attic, which as they get older the kids could use to study in, would be a good idea. He really likes it, so it does sound as though they'll be moving in.'

That was all I knew for some time. They did move but I never found out if Steve had bought the house or continued renting.

I asked Mum when she was going out with my siblings again.

'Tomorrow afternoon, Marc. It's been really busy since I left the hospital, so today, I need a bit of a rest.'

'So where is it you're going tomorrow?'

'We'll be taking them to the cinema. There's a film suitable for children – young ones, I mean. I know Steve won't enjoy it much, nor would you, but the kids will love it as well as all the popcorn and ice cream.

'I expect you're pleased that Loretta is coming on her own tonight. I'm so grateful for how she helped me, and to you for taking control of a difficult situation. You're still young to deal with issues around mental health and you did brilliantly. I'm so proud of you. If you hadn't been there and sat with me that afternoon and heard me talking and talking about my past, goodness knows what might have happened. You listened to me and were mature enough to decide to ring my sister. It was so lucky for me that Loretta was able to organise everything and get me admitted to the hospital so quickly. I want you to know just how proud I am of you and how much I love you. Now, I'm going back up to rest a bit, Marc. See you later.'

I decided that I would also go back up and found a book I wanted to read. After propping myself up on the bed, within minutes, I was completely absorbed in an exciting story about criminal gangs and the police. About half an hour later, I heard Gran going downstairs. A little later on, she came back up and went into Mum's room.

I couldn't hear what Mum was saying, but I did hear Gran telling her she would bring her up some tea and toast.

Mum had seemed very tired that morning, which puzzled me. After all, she had gone to bed almost as soon as her sisters had left, which was only about eight thirty.

Gran called both of us to come down as lunch was nearly ready. I realised I was hungry as I had been so caught up in my book that I never had breakfast. Mum came into the kitchen a couple of minutes after me.

Gran was whipping up eggs and she told us that they were going to be turned into tomato, ham and cheese omelettes if we agreed. That took little persuasion and I quickly laid the kitchen table before she passed the first one to me. Mine was quite a large one, while Mum and Gran shared the second one. I certainly enjoyed it and so did Mum – Gran always made the best omelettes.

Mum was chatting away, but that didn't stop me noticing she was still very pale. Maybe she'd been doing too much since she'd only just come out of hospital. It was only a few days ago, after all. Perhaps it was a good thing that she was staying in today.

When she went upstairs again, she took another large glass of water with her instead of a cup of tea. I didn't know then about all the medication that she had to take more than once a day.

'I'm going to shower and wash my hair,' she told us. As Loretta was not due for another three hours, I guessed that she was going to lie down again.

Gran told me that, before my aunt arrived, we should make it look as though we still had some cooking to do.

'Why, Gran? There's still loads of stuff left over from last night in the fridge,' I protested.

'Because I want those two to have some time together alone – I think it would do them good. I'm sure that they will feel comfortable being able to chat without anyone else in the room with them for a while.'

She began pulling a few things out of the fridge: chicken thighs, an onion, mushrooms, carrots, leeks and a few potatoes. I asked if she wanted some help, but she said, 'It's going to be a casserole and that I find easy to make, so why don't you go for a walk? The sun's shining, even though it's not that warm now.'

After agreeing with her, I put on some boots and a jacket and went outside. My feet began brushing against the golden leaves that had fallen from the trees. They were dry and crisp, and I loved the crunchy sound they made as I walked on them. When I looked up through the branches of the trees, I could see a blue sky with gleaming streaks of sunshine above my head, which made me want to walk further. I must have covered more than a mile, and when I finally got back to Gran's, it was just before Auntie Loretta was due to arrive.

Mum was still upstairs and I wanted to make sure she was awake before I had a shower too. When I knocked on her door, she told me to come in. She was lying on the bed, a book open beside her. I asked her if she was more rested now. She said she was fine and was looking forward to seeing her closest sister. Perhaps it was a brief tightening of her jaw and a tiny muscle twitching above her cheekbones that made me feel that maybe she wasn't OK.

'I decided to take a long bath so I'd better get dressed now.'

She certainly looked a lot better when she came down wearing make-up, smartly dressed and smiling. But however good she was looking then, that didn't take away the feeling I had got upstairs. We were all in the kitchen when we heard Loretta's car pulling up.

'You take her into the sitting room while we finish off the tea,' said Gran, though I knew she had it all ready to take to the table.

Loretta told us that she could smell the casserole even before she came through the front door and knew that it would be delicious.

'Oh,' said Gran, 'it will take a while yet to get it ready.'

We both laughed at this subterfuge as Mum and her sister went into the sitting room.

'It was her resting for the whole day that got her looking better,' Gran confided after I mentioned how tired Mum looked just before she had got dressed and put her make-up on. She tried to explain that Mum being in hospital for so long meant that she hadn't got used to helping in the kitchen or going shopping – 'She's been doing quite a lot during these first few days since she came here. Her energy will gradually come back, so don't you worry, Marc. Being in hospital for so long, she hasn't been used to doing anything much. The patients all have to go to bed early, which is why she still does now.'

I believed Gran then, and for a long time, I didn't

understand what had caused my mum to often look so tired and sleepy. Back then, I hadn't been told about the meds she was now on. They were a class of drugs that was used in those days to treat patients with depression as well as nervous-system disorders. I have since learned that they are seldom used now as, over the years, so many people have had serious side effects and there are much better drugs available.

Mum continued to have days when she looked good but then there were others when her face was pale and her eyes drooped with fatigue. Despite Gran's reassurances, this troubled me.

25

That evening, after Mum and Loretta had spent some time together, Gran went into the sitting room to let them know that our tea was just about ready. I had laid the table so all we had to do was bring in the warm plates and the steaming casserole pot. Of course, both of them got up and followed her into the kitchen so that they could help bring everything in.

'Must have taken you ages, Mum,' Loretta said and I could tell by her smile that she knew the food was ready to be served when she came in. I was pretty sure that she was pleased that Gran had used the excuse of having to stay in the kitchen so that she could have some time alone with Mum. But then Loretta must have known her mother very well.

We all sat down together to eat and dug into the casserole dish with serving spoons to fill our plates. It was so delicious that we all wanted a second helping.

'She's always been a good cook,' Loretta said, 'and thank

goodness she taught us all how to make tasty meals as well as baking too.'

That explained why Mum was very good at cooking.

We all chatted away at the table long after we had finished our meal but it was Mum who went into the kitchen to bring out some biscuits and cheese as well as leftover cake. She had also made some coffee.

Not long after that, Loretta told us that it was about time she went home. We all went out with her and waited until her car began pulling away. The evenings were definitely getting colder and it was already dark. Above us, there were misty clouds. We hurried back inside and Gran turned up the central heating.

Mum helped Gran clear everything away after her sister had gone. Then the three of us stayed in the sitting room for a short while and watched some of the news on TV before we went up to bed.

* * *

The next day, Mum was going out early to see my siblings and I realised then that Gran and I were not going to church as we often did on Sunday mornings. Not that it bothered me. To my surprise, Mum was already up and in the kitchen, baking a fruit tart.

'It's for our desert when I get back from the film,' she told me when she noticed me watching curiously.

'I'm going to make a roast for us all later on, but let's

have something to eat before you go out,' said Gran.

We all sat in the kitchen and had some bacon sandwiches and Mum drank coffee with hers while Gran and I chose tea. No wonder my siblings missed Mum's cooking, especially as my grandmother had taught her so well.

Around one o'clock, Steve turned up with my little brother and sister sitting in the back of the car. Of course, Gran went out with Mum so that she could chat to her grandchildren. She did say to Steve that he could come over with them one weekend if he liked and she would have a meal ready for them all. I dreaded the idea of that, but little did I know that the invitation was never going to happen.

While Mum was out, I told Gran that I would get my homework done. I remembered how kind my maths teacher had been when he heard about my mother coming home and how he had let me have a few days off from homework. I didn't want him to think that I was using that as an excuse again.

Much as I loved being with Mum, she also had her own life where she spent time with her sisters as well as Steve and my siblings. There were friends as well who had phoned, hoping to see her as well.

Steve must have brought her straight back after the film ended. As I was finishing off my homework, I saw through the window that his car was pulling up. His window was down and whatever he said got her smiling. She stood there and watched him turn the car around and then waved at them all.

I was waiting at the door for her by then and she looked

happy when she stepped in and thanked me for holding it open.

'The kids loved that Disney film,' she said.

'Did you and Steve enjoy it too?' I asked with a grin.

'Well, let's just say we enjoyed seeing our kids enjoying it!' she laughed.

Even Gran looked amused when she joined us in the hall to see how Mum's day had gone.

Mum hadn't given any hints that she was considering going back to Steve. In fact, she kept telling Gran and me that she was enjoying being with us, but I kept wondering how long she would stay. It was obvious that she loved seeing her younger ones too and, judging by her mood and her contented state after being with him, Steve as well. In the back of my mind – and almost certainly her whole family thought the same too – I believed that he was planning to get her to live with him again.

26

Although winter was not far off, there were times when Mum and I were still able to sit outside. We pulled on thick jumpers and warm woollen socks, which fitted snugly inside our boots, to take our mugs of coffee outside and sit together on Gran's wooden bench, close to the back door. There was still some warmth in the daytime, although as the evening approached, it became much cooler. As we sat together in the garden, we imagined how, in only a few months, the spring would look so beautiful as the daffodils and snowdrops started popping up and buds would turn into green leaves to adorn the now soon-to-be-bare trees. Mum said it was all so peaceful and how she always enjoyed studying nature there.

Some of the shrubs had lost their flowers but they were still green and the holly was forming berries that would be red by Christmas. Mum looked up at the tree, which had grown so much taller since she had lived there as a child. She told me that it was Grandad who had put in so many plants.

He knew Gran loved colour so he tried to plant shrubs that would provide colour throughout the year, but it was this tree that was his favourite. During the late autumn, the wind had strewn the lawn with deep-golden leaves, but until winter came in full, there would still be many of them on its canopy of branches.

Mum got us smiling and laughing at these little stories but then there were other times out there in the garden when she seemed more morose and we just sat together in silence. Occasionally, she told me a bit about her therapy. One Saturday morning, she said how good the therapist was and how it was helping her a great deal. She had been to see him the day before and she was very upbeat. But she never did mention all the meds she was on. It was quite a while before I learned that she was on them at all and it was this medication that I blame for what happened to her a long time later. To be fair, the treatment was considered safe and very helpful for patients with her symptoms back then. It took some time for them to be discredited.

One afternoon when I had come back from school, we went into the garden again, Mum with her coffee and me with a mug of tea and a plate of sandwiches as I was always hungry when I got home. She told me that she had been discussing my real father with her therapist that morning. I was immediately alert and immensely curious.

'I've decided that I will visit your father's family very soon,' she announced.

I was shocked, I'll admit, but it also made me happy for

her. As I've said earlier, I had been to see my father's family a few times and had really enjoyed my visits there. I was also friends with my cousins, who were more or less the same age as me.

'I think you'll really enjoy seeing them, Mum. Remember how nice Uncle Kevin was when he visited you at the old house? It was so good of him to come back again the next Saturday and then, after talking to you, he took me to visit my other grandmother. I could hardly believe that she was so pleased to see me and she had gathered most of the family in her home, all wanting to meet me.'

As I finished reminiscing, I realised that not only was Mum silent, but she was looking rather puzzled, which seriously concerned me.

'Don't you remember his visit, Mum? I know you seemed to enjoy seeing him.'

'No, I don't think I do,' she said hesitantly and then asked when it was that he had been over to see us.

'Some time ago. I came back from school and was surprised to see a man I didn't know standing in our kitchen. You seemed pretty cheerful as you were making tea for him.'

'I can't remember that day at all, Marc,' she told me.

I could tell that she was bothered about this.

'Well, Mum, it was not that long before you got so ill,' I quickly said. 'I mean, that was the time when you were a bit forgetful, so don't worry about it. Anyway, I'm sure they would love you to come and see them.'

I noticed the blankness in her eyes again; the same look

that had caused me to ring Auntie Loretta that day. Of course, I was worried, but I still managed to keep a smile on my face as I decided to tell her why she might have forgotten a few things.

Then I suddenly remembered the huge row that Mum had had with Steve. The one that had scared me so much and was the reason why I didn't want to stay in the house anymore. It was Mum's friend Eve who had told her to come over as fast as she could when Mum phoned to ask if we could stay.

I told Mum what I had just remembered and how Uncle Kevin had been over just after that terrible row so it was hardly surprising that his visit must have slipped from her mind. 'It was not that long before the first time you went to Eve, Mum. It was such a traumatic time, no wonder you forgot.' Hearing this, she looked happier and so I continued, 'With all those arguments with Steve going on, I shouldn't think you had enough space in your head to fit in any nice memories!'

She laughed a little at this and told me I was right, but that she hadn't forgotten us leaving and going to Eve's. I was glad that the blankness in her eyes had disappeared and I could see that she was looking much more at ease.

'Well, Marc, you'd better start telling me all about the day your uncle took you to his family. I'd like to know as much as I can about them before I go to visit them.'

'While you were in hospital, I went over to see them several times and they were all really welcoming. When I explained to my other grandmother that you were in hospital, she asked what was wrong with you. I was pretty careful in how I answered, especially as I didn't really know myself. She told me before I left that, when you were home and feeling better, she would really like to see you again. Kevin was keen too, Mum. It sounds as though what happened all those years ago hasn't stopped them from wanting you to be part of their family.'

Mum looked surprised as well as reassured by what I had just told her.

'I can hardly believe it. It was over thirteen years ago when your father died, but I felt that my mother-in-law thought her son's death was all my fault. At the funeral, she just couldn't look at me. Oh, Marc, I'm trying to get back all the memories that have gone from my mind. I just don't want you to start feeling worried about my forgetfulness. For some reason, I'm able to vividly remember some things but I've completely blocked out others.'

As I had heard what Mum had kept saying before she went into hospital, I understood that some of her worst memories were trapped in her mind.

'No doubt I've forgotten Kevin's niceness and there are other things as well,' she said. 'It's a good thing you told me about his visit, especially if I'm going to see them all.'

I couldn't help smiling then – I sensed that the therapist had got Mum making plans to deal with her guilt about the past.

'I think I understand what you mean, Mum, and don't

worry about it being difficult – they want to see you, they really do.'

'Well, to be honest, my therapist knows all about that and he's been helping me to get some of my lost memories back in my mind.'

Years later, I researched more about how electric-shock treatment affected the brain. I could then understand how patients on those wards must have forgotten a lot. Perhaps it was the memories that upset them the most that disappeared. Well, at least I hoped so.

It was hearing how the therapist was helping her that made me decide to tell Mum a bit more so that she might be able to see it all in her mind.

Tell her what Kevin looked like, my inner voice said to me.

'You know, Mum, when I saw Kevin for the first time, it was as if I had seen him before. Who was he, I wondered? And then I realised that he looked so like my real father from the photos I had seen.'

It's a good thing that Mum didn't ask how I had seen those photos before I visited my father's family. She would have been none too pleased that my uncle had shown them to me a couple of years ago. But she just looked at me without saying a word. No doubt she was waiting for me to say something else so I went on talking about the day when Auntie Loretta took her to see the hospital doctor.

'I know what was in your mind when I was sitting with you before I rang Loretta. You hadn't forgotten about my father at all, Mum, but as you talked about him, you sounded so upset.'

'Oh, I never forgot him, Marc,' she told me. 'I tried sometimes, but it never worked for me. I've not forgotten that day and I know how I kept repeating things about your father to you. There must have been a reason why I just couldn't stop. I let my therapist know as much about him as I could too.'

'So, when did you decide to meet up with Dad's family?' I asked her gently.

'It was when I was in hospital and I talked about him in therapy. But I'm not ready yet. I need my therapist to help me prepare. I'm still seeing him twice a week for a while longer. Now, tell me about the day Kevin visited.'

'You were standing in the kitchen and he was next to you. You told me he was my Uncle Kevin, my dad's brother. When the two of you were talking, I could tell that you knew each other pretty well some time ago.'

'That's right. I've never forgotten him or the family. I can remember Kevin when your father, who was my boyfriend then, took me to Barnsley to meet the whole family. He was a few years older than your dad and we got on really well. It was some time after that when your father committed suicide. Kevin was devastated as it was he who found him dead in the garage. Imagine how terrible that must have been for him to have to tell his parents that their son had killed himself. No wonder they felt it was partly me who had caused his sadness to be so deep that he no longer wanted to live.'

'But, Mum, Kevin told me that they realised why you had left him when I was a small baby. They all knew you found out when you were pregnant that he had been unfaithful to you, right up to when I was born. Kevin knew first, but he couldn't bring himself to tell the family straight away. But how did you find out about that?'

'Your father sent me a letter telling me and saying how sorry he was. I wasn't well after I had you – it wasn't anything to do with you; sometimes mums get the baby blues, all the hormones flying around – and I couldn't cope so I left him. After the funeral, I believed that I would never be welcome there again. It was fairly soon after I left that your dad killed himself. As for the funeral, of course, I felt so guilty. If only he had waited a while longer, I expect we would have got back together. Although he had had an affair, I never stopped loving him.'

'When Kevin said he was taking me over to meet the family, do you remember that you said you couldn't go because Steve would be back from work soon?'

'No, I still don't remember.'

'You made an excuse not to go, but I remember him saying that his family really did want you to visit. I got in the car with him because I wanted to know more about my real father. When I arrived at my other grandmother's house, she seemed delighted to meet me. Of course, I felt a bit awkward. I could hardly believe that I was seeing my father's family after so long and I had wondered what they would all be like. My grandmother also looked a bit tearful when she saw me.'

'That's because you look like your dad when he was around your age,' said Mum, giving me a big hug. She looked a little sad then before she told me, 'For the few years I knew your other grandmother, I liked her a lot.'

'So, you missed her as well, Mum?'

'Yes, she's a lovely woman. I look forward to getting to know her again.'

27

Mum had been staying at Gran's house for quite some time. It was the December when she reminded me that we were getting close to my grandmother eightieth birthday.

Mum really wanted that day to be as special as possible for Gran, and the sisters had been conferring on how to make this day a real event for their mother. Of course, everyone would want to give her presents and Mum told me that they were thinking about what Gran would like the most.

The sisters all had different ideas of what we should do. After a few days, Loretta got them to agree to have a birthday lunch in a lovely local hotel.

We agreed on lovely presents to get her, a classical pianist to play the music and a cake to celebrate.

Knowing that Gran would turn 80 in just a few weeks, I studied a photo of her when she was much younger. I thought she looked lovely then but she was still so beautiful. Of course, her dark hair had turned grey and she now kept it short but her blue eyes were just as bright. Over the weeks that I had lived with Gran, I had really come to love her and we were very close. To me, she was a really special grandmother.

It was just before Gran's birthday when something happened that wiped out all our happiness and plans.

Something I've never forgotten.

28

It was just two days before Gran's birthday when I woke up at the usual time to get ready for school. I went into the kitchen thinking it would already be nice and warm but it wasn't and nor was there any sign of Gran, which was unusual.

Oh well, I don't have to leave for an hour, I said to myself as I pulled out some bread and put two slices in the toaster. In the fridge, there was plenty of ham to make a toasted sandwich for my breakfast. I put the kettle on to make tea.

Maybe Gran would like a cup of tea brought up to her, I thought. She deserves to be given tea in bed for a change.

Not if she's asleep, silly, my inner voice said.

Soon, I was eating my breakfast at the table. Even so, my ears were alert as I was wondering if Gran and Mum, who were still upstairs, I thought, would wake before I left for school. It was just when I had finished eating that I heard footsteps which told me that it was Mum who was up.

She'll be down soon, I thought, but then I heard her shouting: 'No, no! Mum!'

I didn't understand what was happening, so I rushed up the stairs and saw that Gran's bedroom door was open. *Mum must be in there,* I thought as I moved to the door. I looked in the room and saw that Gran was lying on her side with her eyes still shut. The sound of Mum's shouts and me thundering up the stairs had not woken her. For a moment, I was puzzled but then I saw Mum's hands very gently turn her mother over onto her back. She kept saying 'Mum!' as she placed her hands on her chest and put her face close to Gran's.

The moment she took her hands away and stood up, she saw me standing in the doorway, looking worried.

'Marc, just go down, please,' she told me. 'I'll be with you in a couple of minutes.'

I couldn't bring myself to ask what was going on. I suppose that I must have known but didn't want to say the words aloud. Gran had died. I just couldn't accept the fact that she was no longer breathing. I didn't know what to do and I felt completely numb when I left the landing and went down to the kitchen.

A few minutes later, Mum came down and pulled out one of the high stools next to me to sit on. I could see she'd been crying but was trying to hold in her emotions for me.

'Oh, Marc, I'm sorry I didn't come down with you, but you know what's happened, don't you? She's gone.'

While she sat holding my hand, I realised that I would never be with my grandmother again. The tears flowed and there was nothing I could do to stop them.

'Marc, darling,' Mum said softly as her arm went around

me, 'she didn't suffer at all. Last night, she just went to sleep. When I went into her room, I knew at once that she was never going to wake up, but dying in your sleep is so peaceful and without any fear or pain. I know you two went walking a lot, but her strength must have been leaving her for some time.'

I still couldn't speak as I just couldn't imagine life without Gran.

I could see, as I was sitting close to Mum, that, like me, she was trying not to cry. Once her arms were around me, I leaned against her for comfort and I felt her body tremble with grief. Mum waited a little before she told me that she had rung Auntie Loretta when she was still upstairs.

'Loretta is going to ring the GP and make the necessary arrangements. I just feel he's the one who should come and it will make us feel a little easier as he's the same doctor who looked after your grandad.'

'Did he die in that same bed as well?' I asked, curiously.

'No, he didn't die here. He was taken to hospital. And like your gran, luckily, he died in his sleep.'

That must have been awful for Gran, I thought, but I stopped myself saying this for Gran's loss would have been dreadful for Mum too.

'Is Auntie Loretta coming over, Mum?'

'She'll be here as soon as she can. She has some work that she needs to finish quickly and then she'll be with us.'

Mum had gone very pale again. I knew that she was doing her best not to show how upset she really was. A sudden horror descended on me: could this cause her to have another breakdown? She was still seeing her therapist, which meant that she was not completely well, and Gran had been such a rock for her too. Would she cope?

I tried not to keep crying but my gran was such a loss. Since I had been with her, she had become so important to me. It was her love and calmness that made me feel safe with her. My school work had got so much better too when I was with her.

Suddenly, I looked up at the clock: school had opened just over an hour ago.

'Look at the time, Mum!'

But I couldn't bear to go to school that morning. I was also thinking that I didn't want Mum to be sat on her own while she waited for the doctor and Loretta to come.

Mum agreed straight away to me staying there and then rang the school to tell them what had happened and how upset we both were. The head told her that he was very sorry and, of course, he wouldn't expect me to be able to attend class. He also said that I would probably need to stay off for a few days.

Mum was still trying hard not to cry in front of me and asked if we could sit outside for a while.

'I know it's cold out there, but fresh air might help a little and I could make us some nice hot tea,' I said.

She nodded.

Luckily, my coat was hanging in the hall – I couldn't have made myself go up those stairs again, not with Gran's door standing open.

I can remember us sitting outside, watching two squirrels running up and down my grandfather's tree.

It was seeing the two grey squirrels that made us stop walking and watch them springing over the thick tree roots, although as soon as they knew we were watching them, they scrambled up the tree as fast as they could, round and round its trunk. We laughed a little and somehow it helped us relax from the sadness of the day. Going into the house with none of Gran's comforting smells of cooking hit us and Mum hurried off to make sandwiches. Loretta came back much later – I think that she wanted to leave us together for a while. She certainly wouldn't have left Mum to deal with both the doctor and the undertaker had she not been up to it. As the eldest daughter, it might have been Loretta's role, but perhaps she wanted Mum to get her confidence back while knowing she was there, should she need her.

You might think this is odd, but I have no idea how long it took for the doctor to come, but a while later, the undertaker arrived with a coffin. By then, Auntie Loretta had been busy making calls and taking charge. As soon as the doorbell rang, announcing the undertakers' arrival, Loretta took me out into the garden again, telling Mum that it would be too much for me. Knowing they were in the house had us all in tears. Loretta was hugging me and Mum at the same time and, try as I might, I couldn't stop crying.

Mum must have called Eve and asked if I could go over for the evening: 'All this talk about the funeral and whether it should be a burial or a cremation will be upsetting for him. He's taken it badly.'

Eve arrived almost immediately. She hugged Mum and

me tightly and asked if I would like a pizza and film evening at her house while the aunts talked about the funeral. I felt unsure but relieved once I saw Mum was nodding her head and encouraging me to go.

'No school tomorrow, so do go, Marc,' she told me.

With that encouragement, I grabbed my coat.

I spent the evening with Eve and she chose the perfect movie – not sad, not too frivolous, but really interesting. The story had my full attention and, for a few hours, I escaped into a different world.

But a picture of Gran kept popping into my head. I remember the way she often hugged me, especially when she had come back from visiting Mum in hospital. I missed her so much. In fact, I missed her a lot when I was in my teens, but even now, after all these years, she often appears in my dreams or my memories. It's as if we are still together and that comforts me and I smile.

There are other memories of my life that have a knack of spinning around in my head, but they don't make me smile at all. If only she had lived a few years longer, she might have helped me sort out my teenage years. Then I would never have made all the bad mistakes that caused me so much trouble and caused me so much trauma for the rest of my life. I certainly missed her in those early years – and I still do. She was the kindest person I ever knew, who radiated warmth and affection to me. Just that love of hers would have saved me from myself.

29

Just after we had finished our tea, Eve kept going to the window and looking up at the sky. I heard her gasp and then, with a smile, she said, 'Marc, let's put on our jackets and go outside. There's something wonderful I want you to see. It's much better being out there than just looking through these windows up at the sky.'

Out we went into that cold but clear night. It was then that I saw the bright full moon peeking through wisps of retreating clouds in the dark sky above us. We watched it emerge into full view and, somehow, it seemed so different from the usual evening sky. Eve told me to keep looking up as the last vestiges of cloud moved away from the edges of that bright and perfectly round golden moon. I then turned my attention to the array of stars shimmering across the sky. It was their intense illumination that amazed me – I had never seen such glowing stars before.

'They're letting us know that there's peace up there,

don't you think, Marc?' I heard Eve murmur in her soft voice.

'I think every star is telling us that – maybe Gran asked them to send us a message,' I said.

I felt Eve's hand being placed gently on my shoulder, which made me look up at her with a beaming smile.

'That was why I wanted you to come out,' she said. 'It's rare to see the sky like this and I just knew that you'd love it.'

Eve was right: looking up at that sky helped me feel so much calmer and I really did believe that Gran had sent me a message. I think that Eve was relieved that, after being with her for that evening, I seemed far less distraught than when she had picked me up in her car and brought me to her home. I'm certain now that she had known that, when Gran died in the night, there would be a full moon the following evening. I had felt so devastated sitting out in the garden when I heard the ambulance taking my grandmother away. I might have tried not to show how I felt, but losing the one person who had been so good to me made me feel a deep sense of loss and emptiness.

I suspect Eve must have explained about the full moon and those brilliant stars to Mum when they arranged for me to go there. I had been in the church choir some time ago and they both knew that we had been taught to believe that heaven was above us in the sky. Mum would have been pleased that there was a clear sky that night, allowing Eve to show me that moon and the stars and imagine my grandmother was in heaven.

I was 13 and the evening that I had spent with Eve, our

family friend, helped me begin processing my first ever loss. She took me home and, after saying her hellos and offering condolences, she hugged Mum. Seeing the family was still in discussion, she just said, 'Remember, if you or Marc find it hard staying here, your rooms are ready with me.'

Mum's eyes welled up as they exchanged another hug.

'Let's see how we go,' she said.

30

Knowing all the aunts were coming back to the house the following afternoon after work, Eve rang and offered to take me to the cinema: 'There's a new film called *Superman* and I'm sure you would you like it. How about it, Marc?'

'I really would love to go, Eve – my friends say it's brilliant,' I said, although I did wonder if she would enjoy it.

I was pretty sure that she and Mum had arranged this outing to give the sisters time to make plans. Although I knew they wouldn't be staying late, Eve insisted we went to McDonald's afterwards, which was a real treat. Once we had finished eating and chatting about the film, she said that, although she was really enjoying the evening, she had to work the next day and so we should head home. I think she might have been a bit surprised when we arrived at Gran's house and saw Mum come flying out of the front door to meet us. That got Eve laughing as she jumped out of the car.

'Is there anything I can do for you?' she laughed once my mother was beside her.

'I'm all right, but my sisters and I have been making plans and we need to talk to Marc,' she told her.

As my aunts' cars were all still there, I think they must have been waiting to say hello to me before they went home.

'Well, promise me you'll give me a call if you need some help and I'll come over,' Eve said as she got back in her car.

Once she had driven off, Mum told me that my aunts wouldn't be there much longer. 'They've been waiting to see you before they go, Marc.'

Looking back, I remember that my teenage self, all hyped up by the film and my evening with Eve, really didn't want to sit chatting with my aunts. As it wasn't that late, I could hardly say I was tired and wanted to go to bed, though.

'I'll go in, Mum,' I said.

'They'll be off soon and I want to hear all about this film,' she told me.

So, I did my best to try and look pleased to see everyone as I walked into the sitting room. Not that it was easy for me to come back into Gran's house, especially when I knew that I would never see her again, sitting in her favourite chair.

Aunt Loretta understood me fairly well and, when I walked in with Mum, she looked up and gave me one of her warm smiles then pointed to the spare seat on the little settee next to her. As I sat down, she put her arm around my shoulder and gave me a hug. 'I'm pleased you're here,' she said, which made me smile at Mum, who had taken the chair opposite us.

Loretta knew what a shock it had been to Mum and me when Gran had died during the night and she must have realised that both of us were still quite vulnerable – me because of my youth and Mum because of her mental health. When we had sat outside together, she had seen how upset I was, so she had told her sisters to let her do most of the talking.

'Hello, love. We're all pleased to see you and I hope you enjoyed the film?'

Loretta may have felt that I would listen to her, but she also knew that she had to be careful when explaining what the sisters had decided. No wonder they all agreed that it would be their eldest sister who would take the lead – she certainly had a knack at making people feel at ease.

I found myself telling them all about looking at the night sky with Eve and how great the film had been that evening. They had all seen the amazing moon as they had driven home and Loretta said they had chatted about it earlier. Mum poured a glass of orange juice from one of the jugs on the table and handed it to me.

'I expect you're a bit thirsty after all the popcorn and McDonald's,' she said as she saw me gulping it down. She glanced at Loretta then and nodded. (Mum told me later that she really hoped that I would be all right with what I was about to hear.)

'I always heard from your gran how pleased she was that you got higher marks at school after you'd been here with her. She loved those walks she had with you too and how you seemed to like the music she listened to.'

When Loretta told me what Gran had said, I felt quite moved.

'Now,' she added, 'remember we talked about music for the party for Gran's birthday?'

I could tell that Mum and her sisters were looking at me to see if I was OK with the way the conversation was heading.

'Now, Marc, let me explain what we have decided to do about the party for Gran's birthday. It's something we all know would have pleased her.'

No doubt I was looking rather puzzled, although Loretta was someone I trusted.

'Well, we've decided to still go to the hotel we booked for the birthday lunch – after all, the deposit's been paid and you know how your gran hated to see good food and money go to waste! There were so many good things our mother did throughout her life and these are the things we want to remember. What we have decided to do is give all the birthday presents to an old people's home. I'm sure you know how pleased your gran would be about that. And remember how we arranged the pianist?'

I nodded.

'Well, he's still coming to play the music she loved. So, how do you feel about the party going ahead?'

'I'll miss her being there with us,' I said hesitantly.

'Of course. We all will. But what we want is to reminisce and retell all the stories about her that we remember from our childhood. There's so much we can recall, but we all have our different memories. Trust me, we'll only tell the happy stories and I'm sure there will be lots to make us smile.'

'Will my cousins be coming as well?' I wanted to know.

'No, we've decided it will be just us and you too, Marc, as you were so close to her. We thought that you might also want to talk about her, but only if you're happy to do this.'

It was only the thought of hearing all about Gran's life that got me agreeing.

31

I find my adult self remembering some of the funerals of family and, more often, friends that I have been to. Thoughts of majestic black hearses carrying coffins at a snail's pace with beautiful wreaths and other floral tributes on top. I can remember standing outside the church talking quietly to other mourners, waiting for the hearse to arrive, followed by more dark cars with close family. But as a boy, I already understood that those hearses that sometimes drove past were taking the person who had died on their last journey. People in the street would often stop and stand as the hearse went by as a mark of respect.

The morning of Gran's funeral, I woke up and instantly thought about the lunch I had agreed to go to. I didn't really want to be there, but I thought going with Mum would help support her. Also, I didn't want to stay in this house on my own. Especially seeing it was Gran's birthday; I would have been even more distressed to be surrounded by her things on my own. All I could think was that she was lying cold in her coffin, and we were going to a party.

Of course, I had to stop thinking like that or I would be in tears again, which wouldn't do Mum or I any good. Another picture came into my head: Gran celebrating her birthday in the hotel with piles of presents in front of her as she beamed when her favourite music was played. How different this day would be if only she had lived to see it.

When I went down, Mum said, 'Let's go into the sitting room,' and she picked up a tray with some tea and bacon sandwiches on it. I didn't feel a bit hungry, but knew I should eat something to get me through the day.

'Now, Marc, I've been thinking, and I want to tell you that I've decided that it will be better for both of us to move out, "don't you think"?'

I was shocked because it was so sudden, but I had to say yes. Even though I had loved being there, the house without Gran was so sad.

'Well, love, are you OK with going to Eve's immediately after lunch? I've spoken to her on the phone and she's said that we're welcome to stay with her.' She looked at me a little sheepishly. 'I also think you'll sleep better when we're there. I can hear you tossing and turning at night, and I can't sleep either.' I keep thinking I hear her getting up in the night. So, could we stay there until maybe I find another place to live?

'I would, Mum,' I managed to say, tears not far away.

'Aunt Betty will drop you off at Eve's after the lunch and

then I'll come back here and pack up everything of ours to bring with me.'

After we had talked a little more, I went upstairs to put on the outfit I had chosen for the party. I gathered all my clothes and stuff and put them all on the bed.

Being my last day in the place that I had loved all my life made me feel so sad.

I couldn't help looking at Gran's bedroom door when I left my room, which made me feel even worse.

Once Mum and I were on our way to the hotel, I worried about what the topics of conversation would be. To my relief, instead of hearing about a funeral, it was an occasion full of amusing stories about their childhoods, all the mischief they got up to, and their parents. All of them recalled being my age and how they, too, sought to be treated differently once they were in their teens. Being allowed to stay out a bit later, getting their first pair of heels and even the fight to be allowed to wear a pale lipstick. It managed to get us all laughing and I wondered, if they had been boys, would their parents have been so strict?

I could tell by the way they were looking at me that I was being encouraged to say something, but there was no direct pressure from any of them.

I did tell them that I hadn't been up to as much mischief as they had. That got a good laugh, which put a bit of a smile on my face. It encouraged me too, so I then talked about my walks with Gran, which had got me liking the countryside even more, and she was really knowledgeable about trees, birds and the small animals we saw. Almost on queue, the piano player, who had refused to take money, came in. Mum had already sent him a list of music that her mother had liked, and he had a lot of music scores with him. He sat at the piano and, with a flourish, went straight into a very familiar Gershwin song, 'Someone To Watch Over Me'. Everyone went silent as they had all grown up with that tune because it was Gran's favourite.

After the lunch, I felt much calmer and it had been a lovely time for the family to share their memories. I was actually so glad I had been included. Once I was at Eve's house, life carried on as normal until the day of Gran's funeral arrived.

Mum and my aunts did ask me if I really wanted to go, but I insisted that I owed it to Gran.

I had heard a little bit about my father's funeral, but this was different. His was a tragic occasion because he had killed himself, whereas Gran had lived a long life. The musician who played at the party also played some of her favourite pieces on the church organ. When the coffin was brought out, we heard him play, 'Someone To Watch Over Me'. Hearing it ring through the church on that mighty organ put tears in my eyes and I saw Mum turn her head towards me. Fat tears were running down her cheeks too. Aunty Betty passed a packet of tissues down the front pew and all the sisters were wiping away tears as they said goodbye to their mother.

But it was Steve, who was sitting with me behind the sisters, who put his arm around me when we saw the coffin proceed down the aisle on the shoulders of the men in black morning suits.

'Stay with me, Marc. You've been very brave, but let her daughters go to the graveside.'

'What about Mum? Won't she mind?'

'She asked me to look after you.'

While I stood, his large hand took one of mine and he suggested we go and sit in his car. I could still never trust him but I was grateful to him in that moment. I just didn't understand the full ramifications of what that meant at the time.

Once Mum came back to join us, he took us out for a coffee. There was no gathering, no more family, most of Gran's friends had died. It felt like a sad end to such a big part of my life.

32

Now I'm in my late forties, I have many good and some very sad memories about my younger years.

When I reflect back, I also realise that the life I had before I hit my forties was very different from the one I have now.

Shall we just say it's now much calmer.

I now live in a flat that is large enough to house my four-legged friends, which I love more than anything else. Two of them are rather portly staffies who I have to take out for several walks each day, which is good exercise for me as well as them.

Then there's George, my extremely bossy black-and-white cat, who likes to sit on my lap most of the day and every evening when I listen to music or watch TV.

Of course, I do have human friends as well and I'm close to quite a few of them, many of whom I have known for many years.

I know that there are certain details within my story that

might be hard to read. What I would say is that the following pages you are about to read go through some of the problems I encountered after Gran died. Some might shock you, but I am going to be as honest as I can.

I should have known that Mum would go back to Steve. Maybe if Gran had lived longer, she might have made the break a permanent one but that was not to be.

As for me, I know if we'd not lost Gran, I would never have mixed with the wrong crowd; people who got me into so much trouble and led me down such a self-destructive path. If only I had been able to spend the rest of my teenage years living with Mum at Gran's.

It didn't take very long for Mum to decide that she was ready to stop seeing her therapist. Her excuses were multitude. She needed to see her other two children more regularly as well as spending time with me and there were things to sort out with Gran's house. I kept asking her if she was sure that she was feeling completely all right? I wasn't sure that stopping those appointments, which always gave her such a boost, was the right course of action. Even to me, the benefits were visible. But I didn't realise that Mum had already decided that she would go back to Steve when she was ready to. Her plan was not to agree to return to him too soon, and certainly not before Gran's funeral. It wouldn't have pleased her sisters, who had been so supportive of her decision to leave him.

I can understand now why she kept him waiting. He let her know that he wanted her back with him and their children as soon as she left the hospital. Having to wait so long made him as pleasant and helpful as he could possibly be. It would also make the children happy as they missed her and all her wonderful meals. Cooking was not one of Steve's assets, or so my little brother kept telling me.

Not much wonder that she had stopped her hospital meetings. Wasn't it him she had blamed for her breakdown? Her therapist knew that and might try to persuade her to reconsider.

So, I think her real reason for putting an end to her therapy was because she was embarrassed that all her talk about working, looking after herself and staying single meant nothing. Goodness knows what she had said about Steve to her therapist but I'm sure she had spoken about his bad temper, violence and other problems he created in the home.

We stayed at Eve's for several months before Mum finally told me that she was going to go back to him. I almost said I would stay at Eve's if she would let me, but I didn't feel I could say that to her because it would mean her making a long-term commitment. Mum kept disappearing from Eve's house and I knew it was Steve she was seeing and not her friends or her sisters. Through snippets of conversation, I worked out that she was spending a great deal of time with him and their children.

Eve never told me what she thought, though I could guess it didn't please her very much either. She did her best to encourage me academically but, for some reason, I wasn't interested in doing well.

Since I had lost Gran, my mind was far from peaceful. Eve was amazing, though – she encouraged me, getting me listening to music, reading books and getting good marks, and I was happy most of the time. I think I could sense it was going to be short-lived, though.

When Mum finally told me what she had planned on the day of Gran's service, I could tell by her voice that she was expecting both of us to go back there. Sure, I remembered Steve being kind to me more than once, but I hadn't forgotten his other side. So, all I could do was hope that the part of him I disliked wouldn't come out again.

It was when Mum had spoken to me about our new home with such a happy smile on her face that I realised that she must have fallen back in love with him again. That also confirmed to me that she had been spending a lot of time with him whilst I was at school.

Neither of their two children told me anything about them going out together so I bet Steve told them not to. After all, I saw them nearly every day at school and nothing was said.

I had to make up my mind about what to do when Mum told me about going back to Steve. He had been so kind to me and it was around this time that I'd turned 14 and he'd taken just me and Mum out for dinner and given me a great gift, so I was feeling better about him. Doesn't take much at that age, apparently! But maybe I'd not have been so happy had I known Mum's plans to move us back in with him. It's hard to look back at that time and know what I was feeling.

33

When the day came for us to leave Eve's and move back to Steve's, I was full of apprehension. I was certain it was a mistake and that she and I would regret it. However, Mum was so happy that I decided to give it another try.

Mum and I got everything packed up once again. It was a Saturday morning when we finally moved in with him. Eve had said to me privately that she really hoped I would enjoy living with my family and I hoped so too. She also told Mum that we should go over for an evening meal with her when we were free. I had the feeling that Mum would be spending all her time with Steve and their children, although an evening with Eve sounded lovely; I felt so at home there.

I have to say that, when we walked into Steve's new place, I could see that both the kitchen and the large sitting room looked much bigger than the ones in the previous house. I was pretty sure that he must have a cleaner, as everything was really tidy and there wasn't even a tiny bit of dust anywhere. Nor did the kitchen's floor have any marks on it. It seemed to have every modern appliance, including a brand-new dishwasher, which would make cleaning up after meals a lot easier for Mum and me.

The sitting room was furnished with some small pieces from our previous home, such as a coffee table and a small bookcase. I liked the look of the deep-blue lounge suite near the fireplace, which appeared both expensive and comfy. I wasn't sure what I was expecting but it wasn't this.

I had better not sit on the settee with biscuits in my hand, I said to myself and then, when I saw the light-fawn carpeting, *I'll have to leave my shoes in the hall.* I rather liked the look of the large log basket by the fireplace that was nearly full of small pieces of wood and curled-up newspapers. *That would get the fire blazing quickly,* I thought, hoping that it would be lit every cold evening.

My eyes were still just taking it all in when Steve told me to go to see my new bedroom. 'It's the first one on the left at the top of the stairs. So just push the door open and have a look.' He said this with such a friendly smile that I was immediately curious and rushed upstairs. I could hardly believe this time how good it was. It was certainly a lot bigger than the one I had in the other house. Remember how I hadn't got a desk or a table in my old room, which meant I had to do my homework downstairs? It was far from easy there as I got disturbed quite often by the noise around me. Especially when he was shouting or the little ones were screaming. Looking at my new room, I instantly knew it would be much easier to study. There was a proper office chair too and I could imagine myself sitting at that desk, scribbling away. Also, I could now put on my headphones and listen to music on my Walkman while I was working.

When I went back downstairs, I made sure to thank Steve.

'Good. I'm pleased you like it, and as you've said, it's also a place you can work in. I wanted you to still get your good marks at school.'

'I'll do my best!'

When my siblings came in about an hour after we had arrived, they seemed absolutely delighted when they saw the luggage that had arrived with us, still standing in the hall. Their delight to see me too was reassuring.

I couldn't resist asking where they had been, as I saw they were carrying a thick canvas bag between them.

'Swimming in that big indoor swimming pool down the road. We're both learning to swim now and have classes every Saturday,' my sister said. 'Dad says if we can swim, we can all go to Cayton Bay once summer comes.'

I could see Steve looked amused as it was at least two hours' drive away. Still, I would like to go there as well.

'Sounds great. I expect you're both doing well.'

'I swam a length today,' said my sister.

'I almost did too,' said my little brother.

It almost felt like playing happy families again.

34

However I felt about the situation – and I was still feeling a little unsure – I wanted to make the effort for Mum. I didn't want her or Steve to be disappointed if my marks weren't good, so I made myself work quite hard on my homework. When I was in a lesson, I listened carefully to our teachers, though there were times when I couldn't answer any of the questions that I was asked. The teachers, knowing what I had been through recently, tried to encourage me by saying that they understood my not knowing everything they asked yet, and it was probably because I had missed quite a few lessons.

'You'll soon catch up with everyone in the class,' the maths teacher told me, who had known about Mum being in hospital and then Gran's death.

The English teacher said more or less the same and gave me some notes to read.

'Just go through them gradually, and don't rush too much,

Marc,' she said while I was putting them into my backpack as it was time to go home.

I can remember now that, when I got home with my siblings, I would take a mug of tea upstairs. I hardly wanted to leave my room as it was so peaceful there. If I was in the sitting room, I would have to listen to all of them chatting, so once I was finished, I would just lie on my bed and listen to music. I started to spend a lot of time on my own.

What I didn't realise then was that, however much I managed to smile and chat to my brother and sister, underneath those friendly gestures, I was beginning to become a depressed teenager.

I didn't really understand what was wrong with me. In fact, it took quite a long time for me to work out that I was no longer enjoying my life. Looking back, I know I was trying to find meaning in what was happening. I kept telling myself there was nothing wrong about being at Steve's place. After all, Mum was there and so were my siblings, who seemed fond of me. Now, I could say, all these years later, that my younger self wasn't picking up all the signs of me not being completely well. I wasn't capable of that self-awareness at the time. I began to stay in my room much longer than I needed to, because I felt uneasy interacting with everyone downstairs – even with Mum on occasions. I missed the times when both Mum and I had been at Gran's and the three of us would often sit chatting together for hours.

I can remember the life I had with Gran and how, after the funeral, I couldn't stop missing her. Mum and her sisters were so close to Gran, but in Steve's house, I had become different. My siblings wanted my attention quite often but, even then, I couldn't stop feeling lonely. I hardly ever just sat with Mum and we were seldom the only ones in the house. Of course, I wasn't being rational, but I began to think that she didn't want to spend much time with me. I was certainly old enough to meet up with my friends and arrange to do things with them. I had been given so many cards on my birthday I should have realised those kids liked me. Though, for some reason, my feelings didn't acknowledge that. It was after a couple of months at Steve's that I was not far away from needing help. There was a lot going on with not only my life but my friends lives too – we were all breaking apart, finding new friendship groups, and not necessarily good ones in my case, and it was the start of a lot of problems in my life.

Walking home, I saw empty houses and flats where some of my old friends had lived. Since the strikes, new people who had never been near a mine gradually came to live in our small town, as well as in Barnsley. As the mining stopped, different types of work became available in South Yorkshire and different people moved in.

There were still some families whose fathers had to work away in different parts of England so that they could send enough money for their family to live on. I heard Steve saying to Mum that there was so little discipline in the homes without fathers being present; something I found out was true. I saw the difference in friends I had known for ages, especially at break time and after school.

There was an expression in their eyes which told me they were worried. Not that they ever mentioned it. Though there were a few times when one of the boys told us with delight that their father had got a house in the town where he was working, so his family could move there. I felt then that I would be saying goodbye to many boys I knew.

A few old friends, as well as some of the new boys, came over to me in the playground and suggested a few things we could get up to after school. I wish now that I had been more selective about who I mixed with.

I have to admit that I didn't care and made bad choices after Gran had gone. Of course, Mum was good to me, but I don't think she noticed that I wasn't happy. She was so enchanted with the new house and rebuilding her relationship with Steve. She still enjoyed spending time with her sisters as well as some of her friends, but I never invited any of mine over. It created a distance between us that started me down a dark path.

35

I have one indelible memory that is never far from me, although I was only 14 when it happened.

It began soon after I started mixing with the wrong people. Not all of my friends were what you'd call 'bad influences', but there were two boys who were a little older than me who had started at our school just a few weeks into the new term. I didn't know anything about them but I wish I had, then I might have told myself never to mix with them. Sadly, it took me quite a while to realise the harm they brought me and what they were actually about. When we first met, it was a lot of fun – friendly smiles and lots of jokes that got me agreeing to take them around our small town and introduce them to the neighbourhood. Of course, I believed I had just found a couple of new friends, which, after the few years I'd had, actually cheered me up. As these new boys lived in Barnsley, I truly believed they wanted to see some of our town, maybe even go to a café or a few shops, but they just wanted to go and hang out in our local park.

'Come on, let's go there, Marc,' and I reluctantly agreed. I didn't know why they wanted to go to our small park with nothing in it.

I had no idea that one tiny event – one nod of the head – would cause me such a lot of trouble.

When we got there, one of them asked me if the police were ever around the area.

'No, of course not. Why would they come to a park?'

'You know, just to stretch their legs,' he said, which made me laugh. How naive I was…

'We haven't got many of them here anyhow,' I told them.

Hearing that made them glance at each other with small, knowing smiles. If I had been a bit more streetwise then, I might have realised that they had plans; plans that would get us all into trouble.

The next day after school, my two new 'friends' told me they wanted to bring some friends of theirs from Barnsley to the park.

'We'll have a good time there and you'll like our other friends.'

They both insisted it would be a fun evening and, sadly, I believed them. I was so naive and just enjoying feeling a bit happier and 'normal'. I was easy fodder for them but I had no idea at the time.

That afternoon after school, I managed to get my homework done as soon as I was home and then got ready to go out. I knew Steve and my mother were going to one of the new wine bars that Mum liked, so I let them know that I was going out. Luckily, they didn't ask who it was that I was seeing, I think they were just glad that I was seeming a bit happier and getting out a bit as they had clearly seen how down I had been. I know now that Mum was really worried that I had been depressed for quite a long time, and she was sure that meeting up with friends would help in getting me better.

'You have a good time, Marc. I'll ask Joan from next door to come and sit with the kids. Her television is on the blink, so she would love to have the opportunity to watch ours.'

As soon as I got to the park, I realised that things were not quite as good as they seemed. There wasn't actually any trouble on that first evening. Things didn't get really bad for a few weeks. However, it was clear that my new 'friends' were anything but.

There was a small groups of Barnsley boys who were already there when I arrived. One of them carried a box, which he put down on the ground and let us all see inside. There were a number of lighter-fuel canisters. I just thought they were going to us them to fill their lighters to smoke cigarettes.

'You see these? You have to be eighteen to buy them but my dad got them. I told him we were doing an experiment at school! Silly old goat believed me. Now we sure have a good fun evening here,' he announced with a laugh.

'Yes, Billy,' said one. 'I'll have one to fill my lighter first, and another one to get me enjoying the magic. Cigarette first, though.'

As I hadn't seen the boy called Billy before, I had no idea what those canisters were.

I wasn't a smoker, and didn't have any urge to start, so I just stayed at the back of the group.

'Come on, you,' one of my new friends said to me. 'Do you want one?'

'I don't,' was my answer. But I could feel everyone's slightly menacing eyes on me.

'You're Marc, aren't you?' Billy said, raising his eyes to the heavens as he looked at my friends, who must have told Billy my name.

'Well, firstly, you don't have to smoke. Please show him, you two,' Billy said, looking over to my friends. 'I thought you said Marc was a great guy.'

They came over and pulled out a cannister for me then told me to put the bit that goes into the lighter into my mouth and then push down with my teeth and inhale deeply.

'When you stop, the gas will stop. Just keep doing it and you'll start feeling great soon afterwards. So that's all you need to know really.'

And with that, Billy passed it over to me.

'Now, Marc, when you start breathing it in, you'll probably start laughing a bit and then you'll know you're on your way to getting high.' And with that, he turned away and started handing out the rest of the canisters to the others.

Yes, I was naive and young and silly enough to do the same as the others and got sucking. The gas hit my throat immediately, and I felt an instant burning sensation and couldn't stop coughing.

The rest of that evening is all a bit of a blur.

After about a couple of hours, I managed to get home well before Steve and Mum got back. Luckily, the neighbour who was babysitting my brother and sister was fast asleep on the sofa with the television blaring and they themselves had gone up to their rooms in the attic so I went straight to my room. My head was spinning as I collapsed on my bed.

Still, I can't say I hadn't enjoyed myself so my head was all over the place – kind of knowing it was wrong but also having fun and wanting that buzz again. Stupidly, I went out again with them a week later.

Having fun helped to convince me that there was nothing wrong in what we were doing. I knew Billy had money, as he brought everything that we needed and, having some savings from pocket money, I managed to chip in along with the others.

It was on the third night out with them when everything went wrong and that horror that haunts me happened.

Billy, who had his girlfriend with him this time, put down a box of canisters. Then another boy I didn't know who looked about my age turned up with a much larger gas canister of his own. Goodness knows where he had got it. It must have held a massive amount of gas, and the top was much bigger with a wider nozzle. From the way all the guys acted, they didn't seem to know him well either.

I can't remember how everything started but I remember the boy starting to suck the top of his large canister and me telling him to stop.

'Oh, I'll only take small sucks, and besides, I won't clench my teeth, and the air here will take a lot away,' he assured me.

'It's dangerous.'

But he wasn't listening and, even worse, nor were the others. Billy's girlfriend was the only other person trying to get this boy to stop but the rest were just laughing.

Just as I tried again to get him to stop, he collapsed onto the ground.

Billy's girlfriend started screaming.

I knew then that something was seriously wrong. I just hoped he was only unconscious.

There was chaos around me as my two 'friends' glared at me and said loudly, 'You'd better not talk about this.' I was terrified and just remember running away as fast a I could. Everyone else was in shock and doing the same.

I could still hear Billy's girlfriend's screaming ringing in my ears as I ran. Flashes of remembering how my father had killed himself with carbon monoxide sprang into my mind, escalating the situation even further. When I got back to the house, I was sobbing deeply, and I realised that I had peed myself with fear. That's what fright can do. I didn't know what had happened to that boy. Had those Barnsley lads got help, or had they left him there? I was hysterical.

What I didn't know was that I had been followed.

Mum and Steve were out when I got in but my sister was

there watching television with the dozing neighbour beside her. I thought she was engrossed in the film she was watching but she noticed the way I'd come in, in a total tizz as I rushed straight up the stairs and into the bathroom. After I had thrown up and thrown my clothes into the laundry, I went and laid on my bed in the dark.

It must have been about half an hour later that I heard voices downstairs, which told me that Steve and Mum were back. It was Mum who came up to my room and, switching on the light, saw immediately that I had been crying.

'Marc, what's happened to you?' She sat down beside me and put her arm around my shoulders.

Her kindness towards me made even more tears come, and I sobbed loudly as I leaned against her.

'Come on, love. Try and tell me what's upsetting you so much.'

I felt so guilty in that moment – I hadn't told Mum anything about my two new 'friends'. Not only was I upset about what I had seen happen in the park, I was suddenly frightened of those two.

I know Mum could feel I was trembling so she demanded, a bit more strongly, to know what had happened. I couldn't bring myself to even look up at her face.

'Marc, I'm not going to get annoyed with you about what you've been up to this evening. I just want to know what's happened to make you get into this state.'

'I was in the park with some other boys and something terrible happened there,' I managed to sob out.

Mum's arm tightened around me and she pulled me even closer towards her.

'Come on, Marc. Try and tell me what you were doing there, as well as what you saw.'

I was just about stuttering when I managed to get the words 'canisters, and 'sniffing' out. I felt a little relieved when I saw that Mum didn't look annoyed, only concerned. Calmly, she told me to tell her a little more about the canisters. She must have known then that something bad had happened there. But she kept her tender expression on her face as she waited for me to tell her more.

'Don't forget that I used to be a teenager just like you . So that's why I know all about mistakes. My sisters and I made many of them. So, stop worrying and just tell me what happened.'

I gulped a bit and then began to tell her.

'What was horrible, Mum, was that no one there did anything to stop him. Then the two boys I've been friendly with at school got angry with me.'

'Why were they angry with you?'

'Because they didn't want me to tell anyone what had happened. They both said that they would come over here and sort me out if I did. That was why I ran away from them. One of them grabbed me by the throat as he threatened me. I must have been stupid to think they were my friends, Mum.'

I wondered what was going through Mum's head then – she must have been scared and worried, but was she also thinking about my dad?

'Look, Marc, I'll have to let Steve know all about what you've told me. That boy might still be unconscious in the park, or worse. Of course, I can only hope that the other ones did stay and get him home. Still, Steve will have to phone the police. That's not to get you into trouble, but we can't take the risk of that boy still being out there in need of help.'

I dreaded her telling Steve about what had happened and how he might react. It only took a short while for me to find out because, after he had made that phone call, he came up to me. He sat on a chair facing me and explained what he had told the police.

"Two constables have been sent over to the park and will be trying to find him if those others left him there.'

As I was expecting him to show how angry he was with me, I was amazed that he didn't shout or even look angry. I did suspect that he was disappointed with me as I hadn't done anything to help that boy once I had left the park. In Steve's eyes, that was cowardly.

'I know you were frightened of those older boys, Marc, but even so, I'm sure you know now that you should have made that phone call yourself when you came in. But as your Mum said that you were in shock when you ran back here, I can understand you weren't thinking. You're still looking pale.'

The way he said that made me feel a lot better. I didn't know what shock was or felt like, but I know I was struggling. But I managed to calm down enough to get some sleep. I still had to go to school the next day and that filled me with trepidation.

The next morning, Mum put her head around my bedroom door to make sure I was awake. Steve was in the kitchen when I came down and, for once, it was him who got my breakfast ready. I couldn't stop myself from asking if he knew whether the boy had been found and if he was OK. He had to sit me down to tell me that it had been on the news that the boy had been found but he'd sadly died.

He knew the police were coming round later that day to ask me a few questions but made it clear that they weren't blaming me for what happened – apparently, other witnesses had confirmed that they'd seen me trying to get the boy to stop – but I was still devastated.

I can still remember that day so clearly. I was so nervous when classes ended at break time and I had to go into the playground where my 'friends' were. Luckily, they were nowhere to be seen and, for one of the few times, I was so grateful to my siblings for looking out for me. But I knew there was a difficult afternoon in store for me when I got home.

When I arrived at the house, Mum was there to open the door for me and to try to offer me some reassurance before the police came. And when they did, it was at least better than I had expected. It was true, I wasn't to blame, but it was still hard to talk about and I felt ashamed. 'You needn't be worried anymore. We have the names and addresses of those two friends of yours, and they are being interviewed now by my inspector,' said one of the police officers who came to take my statement. 'I can tell you one thing:

they will not be in your school again, nor will they be welcome in this town. They were expelled from their school in Barnsley for this type of behaviour and your school will follow that policy too. One of the main reasons I wanted to talk to you is to tell you to stop feeling frightened. That boy Billy was at their old school, and he has also been arrested and all three will be charged.'

It offered me slight relief. And, in fact, I never saw those two boys again. I was told sometime later that they had been in court and had been placed in a youth detention place. I knew I was safe from them, but I was left with so many emotions and questions about myself. It only served to set me on a downward spiral. You might think that part of my story ends there with them. But sadly, it was just the beginning of a very difficult part of my story.

36

During the months since Mum and I had moved back in with Steve, she had appeared fairly content and at peace with the situation, which made me feel more relaxed. We all had meals together as a family and chattered quite a lot. I kept wondering if I would hear another row erupting but there seemed to be no problems between them – that is, until the day he found out what I had been up to with my new 'friends' at the park, and that boy had lost his life.

Mum certainly seemed to have changed a little after that evening. Of course, she had to let Steve know all about it, and I'd felt he'd been quite understanding. But, looking back, he must have forced himself not to show how angry he was. I could tell, though, that he was not far away from wanting to snappily voice his opinions about what I had done.

I also later found out that Steve had kept my brother and sister away from home, with him, so that they wouldn't see the woman in blue coming to the house.

It was obvious Mum knew that Steve was feeling very annoyed about who I had been mixing with as well as sniffing gas. I think he felt that it was all too much, and as he wasn't there when the police arrived, he might not have known that I tried to stop the boy in the first place. Whatever it was, it was the real turning point in both his and my, and his and my mum's, relationship. He told her he needed to be stricter with me; something I know my mum felt really uneasy about. I'd only just lost my gran and I think she was trying to give me the space to act out a bit but always hoping I'd just be OK. Steve didn't give me that grace – he made it clear I needed to be supervised more closely, my friends vetted, and to be kept out of trouble. Despite everything he had done, it was clear he was trying to teach me a lesson and make the power he had over me, Mum and the household felt. I didn't know what to think – I was angry, at him, the situation, but I also felt so guilty about what had happened that I didn't stop to question him.

Steve had never bothered before to ask where I was going when I went out or who I was meeting. He didn't seem to care and so I didn't feel the need to tell him. But after the police came, he let me know that, in future, I was to come straight home from school. Under no circumstances was I to go anywhere without informing them where I was going and who I would be going with. I would need his permission to go anywhere, not just Mum's. From his point of view, he told Mum that I had been breaking the law and that they, as a couple, had to make sure that never happened again.

I overheard him saying to Mum, 'They've always been good children, and we don't want them to know what their older brother is like.' Hearing that upset me a bit, but I bet it also made my Mum feel more worried about me again and how Steve treated me so differently to 'their' kids. From what he had said, it was becoming clear that he didn't see me as his son and, after this incident, never would.

It was a strange time – I wondered what my mum must be thinking: if their lives would change again? If it would disrupt the peace they'd established? If her kids would be split up again if they left? If it would lead to her becoming ill again? I know she'd worked so hard to find peace and some comfort since Gran had died, and I didn't want to be the cause of any pain.

But it didn't mean I was happy with the situation either. It must have been at least a couple of months after the policewoman's visit that I started to get extremely fed up and frustrated with the severity of Steve's rules. I had made myself stick to them for what seemed like ages, and I certainly felt I had learned my lesson. I was constantly hoping that he would begin to let me have more freedom, so that I could meet up outside of school with some of my friends. But there was no sign of this happening. Whenever I asked him, he replied, 'Not yet.' How long was he going to punish me for this? I didn't dare ask him that question. My schoolwork was actually suffering as I was so bored and tired of his oppressive rules. I was starting to feel lonely and depressed, and I resented my other friends for the freedom they had.

I can look back now and try to understand it all a bit better, and it makes it a bit easier for me. But I do think Steve's treatment was extreme. I'd been through so much. It was only right if I acted out a little or needed more help to cope. But I realise now that he had never forgotten that I hadn't rung the police myself to tell them about that boy. It was as though he had never forgiven me about that lack of what he saw as decency.

In retrospect, I was only 14 years old. If I had been a couple of years older, I wouldn't have been so frightened of those boys and I am sure I would have had the courage to let the police know about what was happening in the park. But it's easy to say that in hindsight.

So, back then, I became even more isolated. My mood was becoming darker and more despairing. I tried so hard to fight those feelings, hoping that ignoring them would make them go away. We who believe we have some strength in our minds try our best to hide our depression from ourselves and others. It's only when we are alone that we can't help tears coming. When I sat downstairs at supper time, I managed to force smiles on my face. In other words, those who refuse to be weak cover up their sadness by putting on a show, talking and laughing when they feel nothing but emptiness and sadness inside. During that time, there was nothing I could do to relieve this awful depression and I felt that no one could help me.

I couldn't stop thinking about what my life was like before that dreadful evening. I wished I could get on the bus and go to Barnsley, as I had some cousins there. There was no way

Steve would let me do that, though. As I couldn't go there, I hoped at least I would be able to spend time in the afternoon with my other school mates; people I'd known for years and that Steve knew were decent people. Even that would have made me happier, but I still had to walk back home with my brother and sister. There was no reprieve from this sentence.

My friends didn't say anything but I was left feeling embarrassed and hating my situation even more. Eventually, they just stopped asking me to go out or to walk home with them – I wasn't even allowed to do that – and I was even more isolated.

There seemed to be nothing to dispel my loneliness. I wanted to spend time with boys who were the same age as me and not being able to was making me feel more and more miserable. It was a good thing that I was smart enough to cover it up, as I didn't want Mum to get even more worried than she already was. Steve remained steadfast in sticking by his rules and was often in the kitchen when the three of us arrived home from school. There he was with his big smile, handing me a large mug of tea and sending me off to my room to get my homework done.

During the week, when he and Mum went out, a friend of his came over to help my siblings with their homework. In other words, Steve wanted them to understand that I wasn't to go out, and if I did, they were to tell him. I was literally watched all day, every day.

This was my life at the time, and it went on like that for over a year as I slowly spiralled into the depths of anxiety.

37

During my time of isolation, that night at the park was often on my mind. I had become quite disturbed by what had happened there, and I became even more distressed by Steve's reaction to me since. During that time, I overhead him talking to Mum about me. I could hear everything he was saying. He called me a weak boy, just like my father, who hadn't got enough guts to make a life-saving phone call to the police. I heard Mum trying to make excuses for me, trying to change his mind, but I knew he wasn't interested in listening to her. After everything he knew that I'd been through – the abuse, Gran, the boys in the park – none of it made a difference. Any closeness we'd had after all that had disappeared and I knew it wasn't coming back.

I could tell from the tone of his voice and the distaste with which he uttered each sentence that any vestige of fondness for me had gone, and there was nothing I could do to get it back. I felt miserable, almost despairing. I tried to do what

Gran had taught me: think about something you are looking forward to. I wracked my brains, but what? It dawned on me that there was something: my next birthday, when I was turning fifteen. The first desperate thought that came into my head was that I could leave school and move out, away from Steve.

I know that was rather silly of me. I should have told myself that it couldn't happen because I had no idea where to go, I had no money, no plans. All that hard work I'd put in at school would be for nothing. It was Mum who was able to get me to understand why I had to remain in our home until I was 16. More than once I asked why and she explained about social services, who took the view that young people couldn't leave home until they were 16. And even then, she told me both her and Steve would have to be legally responsible for keeping me safe until I turned 18. There was no point in arguing about it; I knew Mum always told the truth. So, I knew I had to stay at school for another year before I could leave the life I'd known. My mum knew me well – she knew I had always worked hard at school and that the main reason was that I'd always wanted a decent job. 'I'm right, aren't I, Marc?' she said. 'You had better work hard so that you'll get good marks for your last exams, which will help you get the sort of job you want; one where you can progress and eventually make good money.'

Listening to Mum made me look at myself critically. *Stop lying on your bed and listening to music. You had better get on with your homework*. It also motivated me to think that, after I got a job, I would always have money in my pockets.

I guessed that Mum must have asked Steve to cut back on some of his rules so that it would make me a little happier. She thought it was reasonable that I could go to the library after school. Remember, this was the time before the internet so most of my exam study material was only available in libraries. I knew Mum felt that, if I kept doing the best I could at school, it might keep me on a path of academic success. Mum wanted to see me thrive and achieve some good results and, after a while, I started improving. I had focus for the first time in a long time. I know Mum was visibly relieved when she read my end-of-term report.

My fifteenth birthday soon came around and, on that morning, Mum woke me up with a big hug and I knew that she would have sorted out something nice for when I got home from school. The day was a nice mix of happy walks to and from school with my brother and sister, and some good times shared with my classmates. Things were starting to feel a lot better.

When we got home after school, I saw that there were brightly wrapped parcels as well as envelopes with my name emblazoned on the front, on the coffee table. I opened my lovely cards, some of which had five-pound notes in them, all from my aunts, who had written lovely messages inside each card. Of course, there was a parcel from Mum. There were even presents from my siblings and then my last one came from Steve. He, knowing I liked music, had given me tokens so that I could buy some more CDs from the same shop I loved to frequent. I didn't expect Steve to take us out for dinner like he had the year before, but I wasn't too sad. I'd come to expect his cold treatment of me, and I didn't expect my birthday to be much different. And it was still a good day, with a nice celebratory meal followed by a delicious birthday cake.

Mum's present was not a surprise as I had chosen it myself when we'd gone shopping the weekend before. When we got to the shops, I saw exactly what I had been wishing for: a new pair of jeans.

It hardly took a minute for me to select a pair of dark-blue ones and, once I had tried them on in the small changing room, they fitted very well. I told Mum they were exactly what I had wanted, and I was really made up.

'They fit me so well,' I said, and they're not baggy in the backside either.' That made Mum grin at me as we left the shop.

'All right, Marc, Happy birthday. But try and act surprised when you open them on the day!' She winked at me and, with both of us smiling, we walked into the tea shop just a few yards away.

Being with Mum without anyone else there made me feel even happier. In those days, we were rarely alone together so having this time with her to chat was so special. After we got home, I couldn't stop thinking about the way we had been together, which was just how it had been during those weeks Mum and I had been at Gran's. I just wished that we could still have plenty of time together, like we had there.

I was also missing seeing my aunts regularly. I had to admit to myself that my life had changed, but not for the better, and I realised I still hadn't come to terms with the loss of Gran. That same feeling of anxiety bubbled up in me – in fact, it had never really left.

After my birthday, I couldn't stop looking at my calendar, telling myself how long it was going to be until I could leave school. I marked the days leading to the next school holidays.

Those months between my birthday and the end of term passed so slowly. Finally, when I was near the end of that academic year, I told myself that it wasn't going to be long before I could leave. Surely, once I left, I would be walking into the cheerful and productive life that was waiting for me.

38

Time passed and I had to seriously start thinking about getting work for when I left school. Mum said that there would be no rush to move out, as she would still like me to stay at home for a while. Later on, I understood the real reason why she had not really wanted me to leave. At the time, she didn't keep pressing me to stay, nor did she give me any concrete reason for not wanting me to leave. If only I had known how worried she was about her future, of course I wouldn't have left home at that time.

I started to notice that Steve and Mum weren't getting on so well again. They never seemed to row when I was there, but I could sense tension and that things were evidently strained between them. When the whole family were together in one room, there was never anything said that would have given me a hint of discord and they never snapped at each other. But I noticed that there was something different between them. They didn't seem to be as close as before.

When Mum told me she wanted me to stay, the first thing that came into my mind was that I couldn't. I had to get away from this house and the harsh rules. I had to get out and live my own life. I had to get away. I had never voiced that out loud to my mum or Steve, thank goodness, but the thought was ever present in my head. I knew I'd miss being around Mum every day, but my inner voice said, *You're growing up now and you have to sort your own life out.*

My plan was to move to Barnsley. One of my cousins had told me on the phone that there was plenty of work to be found there and had offered to help me. At breakfast, I told Mum of my plans and I remember she was just silent. She never said anything to make me feel that I ought to stay.

It was a strange mix of emotions at the time. I don't know why but I just knew that a day would come when Mum would decide to leave Steve for good. She had a lot to lose – namely the closeness she'd found with my brother and sister – so I knew the decision wouldn't be an easy one and it was likely not to happen soon.

What had never crossed my mind was, if they did separate, Steve could be the one to up and leave both Mum and the kids. I had no idea of that then, considering they'd stayed with him before. But I'd begun to notice that, quite often, he was going out on his own.

'I'm just meeting up with some of my old miner friends,' he'd tell Mum as he left to go out.

I wasn't sure if he was telling the truth, and I didn't ask Mum what she thought. I didn't want her to have any more worries.

When school was nearly finished, Mum knew that I hadn't changed my mind about going to Barnsley. She did understand that it was the best place to look for work and that one of my cousins was going to help me but she wanted me to bide my time. However, seeing how determined I was when school finally finished, Mum very reluctantly said that she would help me find somewhere to live and looked into finding me a room in one of the hostels in Barnsley.

It was so good to know I had her support, and I was excited to be moving on to a different town. My elder cousins had a huge network of friends there so it really felt like a brand-new start.

Alone in my room, I kept telling myself that being away from home would help to get rid of my depression. After all, I hadn't had it at all during the months I had been living with Gran. It was after she died when it seemed that the waves of depression were dominating my moods, and thoughts of the abuse I'd suffered, as well as that boy dying, were never far away.

I think Mum sensed it too – in fact, she told me later that she hoped a new start, away from the sadness of Gran and the isolation I'd been forced into, would bring me some happiness.

Was I apprehensive because some of those lads in the park were from Barnsley? Sure, naturally I was, but my cousins had no knowledge of them so I thought it would be a big enough town for me to avoid contact with them, and after all, the ring leaders were locked up.

It wasn't long before the time came to say goodbye to my old life. I don't remember much of it, saying goodbye to everyone, but I knew it was on a Monday, and I had spent the weekend packing my things. While Mum was driving us there, I really had hope for the first time in a long while. I truly believed that, at last, I could say goodbye to the awful depression that had clouded my mind for such a long time.

Mum had paid my rent for two months, and as she said goodbye she had pressed some notes into my hand, saying my Gran would have wanted me to have it. But I had only been in the hostel for a couple of days when I was lucky enough to find a job in a café. One of my cousins told me that the manager there was looking for another young person to train up. He said he would take me along and see if there was any chance of me getting that position.

When we arrived, my cousin introduced me and explained that I was looking for a job.

'You've come at the right time. One of the staff is leaving at the end of the week. It's always busy here, Marc, but I should think it won't take long for you to learn what to do. I'll train you personally, but the other staff will help you get up to speed.'

I was really pleased that it had all happened that quickly. I went to a phone box and called Mum, who was delighted with the news. I could sense a sadness in her voice but I tried to push it down and enjoy my newfound freedom. In the evening, my cousin and I went out for a couple of drinks to celebrate me getting my new job. I looked older than 16 and the barman never queried it. During that week before I started work, I walked around a lot to get to know the area. In the evenings, I read in my room. I had signed up for the local library and I remember the freedom I felt at being able to go there whenever I liked and take out whatever book I wanted. It was a small thing, but it made me feel happy about the choice I'd made. I was making friends too and saw my cousins quite a bit.

On my first day at the café, the manager welcomed me. He asked one of the others to show me how to work the coffee machine. It didn't take me more than a few minutes before I could do it myself. I have to say I enjoyed the work. During my first day, I felt that it was going to suit me, and after a couple of weeks, the manager kept telling me that I was really useful.

I'd love to say it stayed like that too. If only I had put work first and spent more time with my cousins instead of my new friends who liked to go to the local clubs. The clubs were where my problems began.

* * *

I can still remember what my hostel was like, almost down to the inch. It's ingrained on my memory. I met other boys there, all a similar age; some older, but all of us in a similar position of having left our homes, though some had had no other option but to leave, and had suffered such abuse at the hands of those supposed to love them. Those guys were feeling that same sense of freedom I did, and all they talked about was letting loose and all the great clubs in town. I did think it might be fun going out with them but, as I was seeing my cousins and friends regularly, I didn't go straight away. When I asked my cousins, they just shook their heads – they were more interested in the local pubs, watching football and having a pint or two. But it didn't take me long to find a new form of entertainment.

It was on a week when my friends and cousins were on holiday that my life went wrong. Being alone certainly got me bored. After all, in Gran's home as well as Mum's, I had never been alone for long. I can see my younger self back then, smiling and laughing so that the darkness in my mind was hidden from them.

'I'll be all right now,' I told myself. But when I was in my room alone, I knew that I wasn't.

That realisation made me feel sick. I had believed that, when I left home, I'd be leaving my depression behind but it just followed me. It was right in my room with me, invading every pore. I knew I had to do something to fight against the darkness that kept jumping into my mind.

Go to a doctor and get yourself sorted out, my inner voice told me.

I can't remember now exactly what I said to that doctor. I should think it was all about my lack of sleep as well as me getting depressed. I must have told him quite a lot, though, because he gave me a prescription for Prozac, which would help stop the thoughts and memories that upset me. Another bottle with small tablets was also part of what was prescribed and the doctor told me to take one when I went to bed so that I would get good night's sleep. I can't recall the name, but they sure knocked me out and I had to go to bed earlier and earlier to still be at work for 8 a.m. But although that second one managed to stop me staying awake for hours, what it didn't do was brush away my nightmares. There were several ones I hated that refused to leave me. The worst were the dark ones that had me screaming in my sleep. Then sometimes, worse things happened while I was only half-awake; my eyes kept seeing strange creatures in my room. They finally disappeared through the walls, which, despite the medication, left me unable to get back to sleep. The pills I took in the morning did help me a little, but they couldn't stop those nightmares, which left me tired all the time.

It didn't take me very long to make a huge mistake; one where I was lucky not to go completely crazy.

39

It all happened one night when I went to the local club with some of the boys from my hostel; one where there were a lot of teenagers dancing wildly. It dawned on me that there were also a few fairly young drug dealers around the place and my companions seemed to know them pretty well. As the four of us were coming down the steps into the club, one of them had nodded at those guys and told me they were good dealers. They must have thought that I was there for the same reasons as the other three but I was only in that place for the first time and my eyes were taking it all in.

On one side, I saw a tall, good-looking DJ standing on a high grey block, with a group of girls looking at him adoringly. When he got more wild music going, the dancing moved up a pace.

At the opposite side from the steps was a long wooden bar with stools in front to it. I then followed the others, who were walking towards it, as the crowd kept on dancing manically.

Having only just left Kexbrough a few weeks before, I still wasn't used to drinking much alcohol. At home, I certainly hadn't been allowed to, nor had I been in pubs with any of my friends there. Out with my cousins, I had only drunk the same drinks as them, which were just small glasses of beer or cider. As I hadn't much idea about what was best for me to drink, I just asked for the same rum and Coke that the others ordered. Looking back, I was so naive.

For the first time in my life, I got drunk. That was enough for me to lose all semblance of caution and any common sense that a 16-year-old should be able to exercise. Being so drunk must have been the reason why I only have small fragments of that evening in my memory, which is most probably just as well for me. Still, being rather wobbly on my legs didn't bother the dealers at all. A drunk punter is easier to sell to. I expect they were used to their buyers being like that.

Even now, I wish that I hadn't gone to that club or with those people.

I can only faintly remember about one of the dealers coming over. He asked if I would like to buy some Ecstasy. Of course, he wouldn't have known that I had never even heard of that particular drug. I guess I must have given him the money for them and, instead of just buying one tablet, I bought two. I suppose I must have got another rum and Coke so that I could swallow the first pill easily. Not surprisingly, I don't know when I put a second one into my mouth.

As I said, I didn't know anything about Ecstasy, a drug

which everyone said 'was supposed to make the world brighter'; but, of course, not if two were taken in quick succession.

It must have been when I was dancing – or rather thought I was – that I started hallucinating. Wanting to get away from them, I carried on dancing wildly until I collapsed onto the floor.

It didn't take long for the lads from the hostel to get me up the stairs and then into the dealer's car, jostling me to make sure I stayed awake and didn't pass out.

I can't remember how I got into my room, but even worse is that I still can't recall how I managed to get hold of my sharp penknife and cut my wrists. Even now, I still don't understand why my drugged-up mind wanted to end my life. Thank goodness I had no idea what I was doing. But I still managed to do some serious damage, stabbing the knife into the fleshy part of my arm. There was blood everywhere but I hardly noticed at the time.

I still can't remember phoning Mum, or even why I did? She must have been terrified when my last words to her on the call were, 'Goodbye, Mum. I want you to know I love you.'

The next thing I remember was a frantic knocking at my door. Mum had got to the hostel as fast as she could, having first rung the manager, who was fast asleep but raced out of his home with the keys to get into my room.

Apparently, there was blood all over the floor under the hostel's pay phone and my sheets were streaked with blood. The manager had managed to get into my room before my mum arrived and, luckily, he had bandaged my wrists to stop the bleeding while he waited for the ambulance. I was in and out of consciousness.

'He's been like this since I arrived,' the manager said. 'I suspect it's drink or drugs or both. Now, don't you worry too much. The ambulance will be here soon. I am sure you can go with them.'

Sadly, I was not the manager's first experience of a situation this and wouldn't be his last.

'Your son will probably be in there for a few days until he gets better. Which, of course, he will,' he said to Mum.

I don't know how long it took for me to wake up in my hospital bed. But I can remember that moment quite clearly. When my eyes opened, I saw curtains hanging around me and Mum sat by me in a chair. I know that I heard her voice, but before I could begin to speak, I fell back asleep again. It must have been a nurse who, when my eyes opened more widely and I was more alert, helped me sit up. It was she who also told me I was being looked after in hospital so there was nothing to worry about, and that I would soon I would be walking around and feeling fine. I looked over at the chair and it was empty.

'Was it my mum who was sitting on that chair?'

'Yes, and she's coming back very soon. She's just talking with one of the doctors.

I didn't know what Mum was asking, but she must have let him know that she wanted to take me home once I was ready to leave. He tactfully tried to explain that it might be better for both her and me if I was sent to a different hospital that had a psychiatric ward. He also told her that I would be sectioned until the doctors were certain that I was well enough to leave and not a suicide risk.

My mum must have been heartbroken when he told her that. I know I was shocked when I was well enough to hear that I was being sectioned, but I felt relief as well.

It wasn't just my body that needed to get better; it was my mind that needed help. Hadn't my hands taken hold of that knife so that I could commit suicide?

Mum found out from the doctors that I'd been drinking and had taken drugs too but she told the doctors that she wanted to wait to see how I was for a few days before making any decisions. She certainly didn't like his idea of putting me into a psychiatric ward, where most of the people there would be a lot older than me and some, if it was anything like where she had been, might be really disturbed. She told me later that her memories about how she had spent time in a psychiatric hospital flooded back and she recalled how her physiatrist and therapist helped her think about what she could do to help me. She immediately contacted her therapist and explained what had happened. I still don't know exactly how she managed it, but she arranged for someone who her therapist recommended to visit me.

A couple of days later, a friendly man, who I just assumed was one of the doctors, came over to talk to me. Unlike the other doctors, he sat down by my bedside and told me that he had a few questions to ask.

It took me a little while to find out he was a psychiatrist. Mum had met him just before he came to meet me and she later said she could immediately tell he was the right person to try to understand why I had almost killed myself. There were some quite general questions to begin with, such as what hobbies I had, that made me feel like we were just chatting. Though once we had talked a little more, his questions became a bit more intense, even though his style remained chatty. They were a lot easier to answer than I would have thought, given their nature. One of them was about drugs, and he wanted to find out what medication I was on and also what recreational drugs I had tried.

'You mean taking tablets and cigarettes with stuff in them, do you?'

'No, Marc. Just tablets, seeing that you don't smoke, or do you? Marijuana?' I shook my head.

I might have taken a bit longer to try to explain about the Ecstasy.

'Do you mean you felt you were having fun after taking one?'

'No, it scared me.'

When he asked why I took the other one, all I could do was shrug. He then asked how I had got them, and I told him about how they were being sold in the club. I guess I babbled on a bit, as I must have let him know quite a lot about that place. Of course, being a psychiatrist, he knew all about the problems drugs can cause. That's why he needed to find out how often I had taken them.

'So, you didn't know anything about what would happen if you took those tablets, Marc?'.

I answered truthfully.

'Well, I had seen others taking them. I thought they just made people's dancing really good, you know, not caring about going a bit wild. I joined in because that music was making me want to dance.' The doctor responded with a knowing smile.

'So, the one who sold it to you hadn't seen you before?'

I could see a flash of anger in his eyes when he spoke about the dealer, especially when I told him about my hallucinations, which had made me feel as if I was in a different world.

I could see then that he was scribbling some notes, but I wasn't worried about that.

He then asked what happened after that and I told him about me feeling as if I was falling and how they apparently took me back to the hostel.

It was then that he must have realised I didn't know anything about what I was doing in there, nor did I know about making the call to Mum. I thought the bandages on my wrists were because of them getting the drugs out of my system.

He visited me a couple of times and I knew by then that he was a psychiatrist who was on my side, and he told me if I ever needed help when I was out of hospital, I could get an appointment with him if I needed to.

It was during his second visit when he asked me a question I hadn't expected.

'Are you gay, Marc?'

It was one of those core moments in life that you know you'll never forget, that will be ingrained in your brain forever. I almost flustered, unsure as to what he was asking and why. But I knew it was something I'd been grappling with and had told him that I was unsure how to feel, especially after I'd told him about what had happened on the farm. He was very firm in his response to that and said what that man had done was child abuse and it definitely hadn't meant that I was gay or that it had caused me to become gay. We talked about it for a long time and I felt my head start to clear. He gave me some crucial advice that I am so thankful for to this day.

Number one was not to hide who I was from a friend, my family, and certainly not from myself.

He gave me other help too, such as the best way of letting Mum know. It was a huge moment for me. I realised that I'd not been honest with myself, and a lot of my problems had stemmed from that. So I plucked up the courage to tell Mum on her next visit to the hospital. She just smiled and hugged me and told me she knew but was so proud of me for telling her. A lot of things fell into place for me at that moment.

40

It wasn't until I was back at home, that Mum explained just what had happened over the previous few weeks since my accident. I was very lucky to have had visits from that psychiatrist. It was him who managed to persuade my doctors that I should be allowed to leave, provided I returned to my mother's home, rather than the hostel.

It was only a couple of days since he had visited, when the senior doctor told Mum that I was well enough to go home with her at the weekend. He explained that my psychiatrist's report had reached him, which identified why I had appeared to be both physically and mentally ill. The doctor decided to share the main points with both Mum and me.

Mum was shocked by everything. I hated how scared she looked. She was so sad when she told me I'd looked so ill. It had taken me quite a long time to get any kind of energy back and be awake at all during the day. It was only after the psychiatrist had been visiting me that I had begun to look and feel a lot better. I'd felt so isolated so having someone to talk to, and someone who didn't know me or my past, was such a relief. I was even a little brighter when I chattered to Mum. I could see the happiness and relief on her face and it made me feel better too.

Mum had received quite a lot of feedback from the psychiatrist. Everything apparently centred around the drugs I had been sold in the club. Two Ecstasy tablets taken in quick succession, on top of the anti-depressants I was on, had caused my psychotic episode. That, combined with an excessive amount of spirits, culminated in my collapse. The psychiatrist said that if I'd been taken to hospital, rather than dumped at my hostel, I likely wouldn't have attempted suicide. I'll never know, but it must have been a desperate sight. I was so naive about everything; it was just like sniffing gas at the park. It was never going to lead to anything positive or good.

I thought about those guys from the hostel, the dealer who'd tried to remove me from the club, and any evidence with it. They didn't care about me, just about saving themselves. I felt anger that they had just dumped me at the hostel. Why couldn't they have dropped me at the hospital and said they'd found me lying in the street. I thought back to Steve's words that I was a coward for allowing that boy to die… well, they couldn't have cared less whether I lived or died in my room in the hostel. They were ruthless cowards.

Thank goodness Mum had found the psychiatrist. From then on, I saw him regularly during my time in hospital and he had changed all my medication to try to help with my depression. I was so grateful to him for his help. I would have hated being put into a psychiatric hospital and I was determined to work with him to get better.

As we got into the car, Mum dropped a bombshell. She told me that Steve had left her.

'Where is he now then?' I asked.

Mum explained that he had moved out very recently, and that he had been seeing another woman for quite a while and had gone to live with her.

'Where, Mum?'

'Not round here, love. He's moved over to Sheffield.'

'And my brother and sister, have they gone too?'

'Yes, they have. They asked to go with him so they're staying with Steve and his new partner now. But we've got a good arrangement this time, so your brother and sister will stay with us on weekends and school holidays too.'

I could see pain in her eyes when Mum said that, but there something else too. Relief? Happiness? I know she hated not seeing her kids before but, knowing there were going to be lots of visits, this felt like a really positive move forward for everyone. I wondered if my own therapy had helped Mum revisit some of her own? I don't know, but I was just grateful that we were together.

'Are you OK, Mum?'

'Yes, I'm all right, Marc. Relieved, actually. Those rows and the anger were wearing me down.'

'Does that mean you're not that worried about him going?'

'No, actually, I'm not. I've known for quite a long time about his affair and I was tired of it. I was on the verge of leaving again, especially when he drove you away, love. He was so harsh on you. My priority now is to get your mental health sorted out. I'm so happy you're coming home, and all the aunts are too. I'm not saying that you have to live with me forever, but for the moment, it would be better for you.'

And yes, I felt pleased to be going home with Mum. I knew we would be good for each other, just for the moment. It was exactly what we both needed.

But that is not the end of my story.

Epilogue

Life was so different once I came home from hospital. I was so happy to be home with my mum. I was worried that, with Steve and my siblings leaving she would be feeling very lonely but it was the total opposite. With Steve gone, Mum's sisters felt comfortable visiting again, and their company was welcome to both of us. In fact, I felt safe and comfortable enough to share with them that I was gay.

'Have you got a boyfriend yet, Marc?' one of them asked with such a big grin on her face. My cheeks were burning red with embarrassment but I knew it was said with love and affection. It felt amazing to have their support and acceptance.

'Not yet,' I managed to say. But in my head I'd been wondering about relationships and finding someone I could spend time with. Good times with my mum and aunts aside, it was now time for me to get my life sorted out. I needed to find new friends, both gay and straight. It was time to make a new life for myself.

While I wasn't expecting my luck to change any time soon, all of a sudden, to my surprise it did. One day when I was at a café enjoying a drink, I suddenly heard a female voice behind me.

'Hello, Marc.'

I turned my head and looked over my shoulder to see a pretty girl smiling at me. I recognized her instantly as the girl in the park.

'I'd hoped I'd bump into you again. I always wondered if you were OK, and what happened to you.'

I beckoned her to sit by me which she did. I finally had the opportunity to thank her for telling the police I wasn't involved, and that I'd tried to help. It was an unexpected kindness, but I could tell it meant a lot to her and that she'd been affected by it too. We spoke about what we'd been doing in the few years since, and I felt comfortable enough to tell her about the club and everything that had happened there.

'I heard that it's been closed down since then,' I said.

'Serves those bastards right', Amy replied, with a twinkle in her eye. I couldn't help but smile.

We ended up chatting for a while and I asked her what she did for fun. She caught hold of my arm and told me about a little gay bar which had only just opened. My eyes lit up, I couldn't believe it! We made plans to go there for their big opening night that weekend. It was such a good night, and the owner and his friend were so friendly and welcoming. Amy was great company, and we spoke long into the night as we danced. I had fun for what felt like the first time in so long.

Amy asked if I knew much about AIDS, an illness that seemed to be affecting the gay community in particular. I didn't at that time, but she explained how so many guys of my own age had died from it, as well as a lot of older men. She knew some people personally who'd been affected and you could tell it was hard for her to talk about it but it framed my experience as a young man, newly out in the gay community. In the coming years, as I embraced my identity and sexuality, it was a recurring issue and a sadness that will stay with me forever.

Though we're coming up to the end of my story, I don't want to end on a sad note. In fact, this was the beginning of much happier times for both me and my mum. It all began when one of her sisters invited us both over for lunch. She told Mum that a man named Geoff would also be joining us, who was a good friend of my uncle.

When we arrived and met Geoff, I immediately thought how friendly he seemed. Mum was sat next to Geoff at the table so I could sense my aunt was up to something! But Geoff had a brilliant sense of humour and soon we were all laughing and having a good time. Mum seemed to be very relaxed and happy in his company; I could sense that she was beginning to really like him.

As the years have gone by and I have got to know Geoff really well, I think my aunt made a very good choice on that day. They are a perfect match.

That evening ended with Geoff asking my Mum to go out to dinner with him at his favourite restaurant. She returned home from that dinner date with a sparkle in her eyes that I had never seen before. That same night, I'd been to the local gay bar and met a really nice guy. Things were starting to look up for the two of us.

We went for Sunday lunch with Geoff that weekend. As he was speaking to Mum, I could see that he had a great deal of kindness in him. Mum seemed to glow in his company. Looking back, my gut feelings were absolutely right. My Mum has had the happiest years of her life with him, right up to this day.

* * *

Now we come to the third part of my story. My friends started talking to me about a place called Great Yarmouth in Norfolk, a buzzing seaside town with a wonderful theatre and lots of shops, bars and restaurants. It sounded great – and the best thing about it was that it apparently had a couple of good gay bars.

'Come with us, Marc. We know loads of people there and it would be a great place for you to make a whole new set of friends. You will love it there.'

Within a couple of weeks, we were all packing our bags and on our way to Great Yarmouth for the Summer. I was so excited to be somewhere new. I couldn't wait to go out and find out for myself.

We found a gay bar not far away from where we are staying. I could see it was very different to the small one at home that I had been going to and as soon as I opened the door I could see a lot of couples dancing together and openly sitting with their arms around each other. Other single men were searching around for a new mate or maybe someone to just have a good time with. But we noticed some older males who seemed to be chatting up younger men and didn't exactly look like they had the best of intentions. One of my friends told me that the older men were offering money to entice the younger ones to go off with them.

'I'm staying away from anyone thirty or older,' I said to one of the older men who was trying to chat me up. I thought he would be annoyed but he just laughed and bought me a drink.

As our stay continued and we went back to the club a few times, I saw this same man and he'd often come up to me and buy me a drink. It was strange, but he was always friendly.

I really came to love Great Yarmouth, which led to me staying there for longer than I'd intended. I managed to get work in a couple of the bars over the weekends and some evenings. I was earning enough to pay my rent, eat well and have a pretty good social life.

Even though I was having such a good life there, I often found that I missed Mum. We chatted on the phone regularly but it wasn't enough so I'd go home to see her at least a couple of times a year. Geoff always welcomed me and would take both Mum and I out for a meal to celebrate my return.

We always had a great time together. Each time I went back, I felt more reassured that she was so settled and happy with Geoff. He was so good for her.

As time went by, I became settled into my life in Great Yarmouth. But it wasn't all positive. In fact, the next part of my story is sadly not so pleasant. There came the day when I met someone in a bar who I fell head over heels for. He wasn't much older than me and I was instantly attracted to him. In the early days that we spent together I had to try so hard not to let him know just how hard I had fallen for him. After a couple of weeks of dating, he asked me if I would like to come over to his flat and after that we became a proper couple.

As I said earlier, this was the time of the AIDS epidemic and we were all aware that we had to take precautions to keep us safe. I always made sure I had condoms, though I know other couples stopped using them once they had been together for a while.

It was about a year later when I became unwell. My muscles ached and my throat was constantly sore. I sweated a lot in the night so I thought it was some kind of virus. I was scared and I know it was a feeling felt by all gay men when they became sick.

It was one of my friends, not my partner, I decided to confide in.

'Go to the doctor,' he said. 'You need to get a test'.

I went to a clinic to get tested. I got a call just a few days later asking me to return to the clinic, where the doctor sat me down and told me I had tested positive for HIV. I was alone and numb with fear. But I remember how kind the doctor was, explaining everything to me and that there was treatment to help and that it didn't mean a death sentence. I felt a lot easier when he said that, and knowing that I could still live my life. But I was still sad and upset, and trying to make sense of it all. When my thoughts became clearer, I knew there was only one person who could have given it to me as he was my only partner. That was enough for me to end the relationship.

It didn't take long for me to decide that I wanted to go back up North. I needed to go home and spend time with my friends and family. I wanted to see Mum and my brother and sister, who I was now so much closer to. After everything that had happened to me, I realised I needed to stop running and to appreciate what I had all along. I just wanted a peaceful life with those I cared about around me. I realised I was looking forward to being home and looking up all my old friends.

Now I have a home up there. I am contented, surrounded by my animals who I love and good people who care about me. I also have a fantastic online community of book lovers like me, where I recommend all kinds of books. It fills me with so much joy. I never dreamed I would ever do anything like this, but it's taught me that you never know what life has in store for you and that you're in control of your future.

This is the end of my story for now.

I'm off now to make a cup of tea and walk the dogs.

Thanks for reading.